Oracle ADF Survival Guide

Mastering the Application Development Framework

Sten Vesterli

〈IOUG〉
independent oracle users group

Apress®

Oracle ADF Survival Guide

Sten Vesterli
Værløse, Denmark

ISBN-13 (pbk): 978-1-4842-2819-7   ISBN-13 (electronic): 978-1-4842-2820-3
DOI 10.1007/978-1-4842-2820-3

Library of Congress Control Number: 2017952558

Managing Director: Welmoed Spahr
Editorial Director: Todd Green
Acquisitions Editor: Jonathan Gennick
Development Editor: Laura Berendson
Technical Reviewer: Luc Bors
Coordinating Editor: Jill Balzano
Copy Editor: Brendan Frost

Distributed to the book trade worldwide by Springer Science+Business Media New York, 233 Spring Street, 6th Floor, New York, NY 10013. Phone 1-800-SPRINGER, fax (201) 348-4505, e-mail orders-ny@springer-sbm.com, or visit www.springeronline.com. Apress Media, LLC is a California LLC and the sole member (owner) is Springer Science + Business Media Finance Inc (SSBM Finance Inc). SSBM Finance Inc is a **Delaware** corporation.

For information on translations, please e-mail rights@apress.com, or visit http://www.apress.com/rights-permissions.

Apress titles may be purchased in bulk for academic, corporate, or promotional use. eBook versions and licenses are also available for most titles. For more information, reference our Print and eBook Bulk Sales web page at http://www.apress.com/bulk-sales.

Any source code or other supplementary material referenced by the author in this book is available to readers on GitHub via the book's product page, located at www.apress.com/9781484228197. For more detailed information, please visit http://www.apress.com/source-code.

Printed on acid-free paper

For developers who are solving problems,
not just writing code

Contents at a Glance

About IOUG Press

*IOUG Press is a joint effort by the **Independent Oracle Users Group (the IOUG)** and **Apress** to deliver some of the highest-quality content possible on Oracle Database and related topics. The IOUG is the world's leading, independent organization for professional users of Oracle products. Apress is a leading, independent technical publisher known for developing high-quality, no-fluff content for serious technology professionals. The IOUG and Apress have joined forces in IOUG Press to provide the best content and publishing opportunities to working professionals who use Oracle products.*

Our shared goals include:

- Developing content with excellence
- Helping working professionals to succeed
- Providing authoring and reviewing opportunities
- Networking and raising the profiles of authors and readers

To learn more about Apress, visit our website at **www.apress.com**. Follow the link for IOUG Press to see the great content that is now available on a wide range of topics that matter to those in Oracle's technology sphere.

Visit **www.ioug.org** to learn more about the Independent Oracle Users Group and its mission. Consider joining if you haven't already. Review the many benefits at www.ioug.org/join. Become a member. Get involved with peers. Boost your career.

www.ioug.org/join

Apress®

Contents

About the Author

Sten Vesterli picked up Oracle development as his first job after graduating from the Technical University of Denmark and hasn't looked back since. He has worked with almost every development tool Oracle has produced in the last several decades, including ADF, APEX, JET, Application Developer Cloud Service, JDeveloper, SQL Developer, Oracle Portal, Oracle WebDB, Oracle BPEL, Collaboration Suite, Designer, Forms, Reports, and even Oracle Power Objects.

Sten started sharing his knowledge with a conference presentation in 1997 and has since given hundreds of conference presentations at Oracle OpenWorld and at ODTUG, IOUG, UKOUG, DOAG, DOUG, and other user group conferences around the world. His presentations are highly rated by the participants, and he has received the ODTUG Best Speaker award twice.

Sten has also written numerous articles for Oracle Profit, Oracle Scene, and many other publications. This is Sten's third book on Oracle ADF; before this one, he wrote *Oracle ADF Enterprise Application Development – Made Simple* and *Developing Web Applications with Oracle ADF Essentials*. You can find Sten online at www.vesterli.com, on LinkedIn, and on Twitter as @stenvesterli.

Oracle has recognized Sten's skills as an expert communicator on Oracle technology by awarding him the prestigious title, Oracle ACE Director, carried by only around 100 people in the world.

An independent consultant based in Denmark, Sten works with customers worldwide, helping them get the most from their investment in Oracle software. In his spare time, Sten enjoys triathlons and is working toward his private pilot license.

About the Technical Reviewer

Luc Bors is Partner and Technical Director at eProseed NL and member of the global eProseed CTO Office. He is an Oracle ACE Director and Certified Specialist in Oracle ADF and Oracle MAF and Oracle MCS. With over 20 years of experience as a principal consultant, architect, and trainer, Luc is recognized globally as one of the authorities in his area of expertise.

In his work as consultant, Luc is able to influence customers and to work at a high level in the organization to technically guide projects that can have big impact. Luc has proved his skills in many projects, both in The Netherlands and worldwide (Canada, USA, Denmark, Germany, Belgium, Kuwait).

Luc is the author of the book *Oracle Mobile Application Framework*, published by Oracle Press in 2014. He also regularly writes articles for international magazines, websites, and his personal blog, and he is a frequent presenter at international conferences such as ODTUG KScope, Oracle OpenWorld, and UKOUGtech. In 2011, he was awarded the best speaker award at ODTUG KScope in the Fusion Middleware Track. Luc has participated in the Mobile Beta testing program on several occasions, is a member of the Oracle Mobile Development Customer Advisory Board, and has presented about the Oracle Mobile Application Framework at many conferences.

Acknowledgments

I want to thank Oracle for providing us with Oracle ADF, which is the best tool for rapidly and efficiently producing user-friendly full stack applications. I appreciate that Oracle gives us this powerful technology for free in the form of Oracle ADF Essentials, and that Oracle is continually evolving ADF. With new, even cooler visualizations and the ability to publish ADF business logic as REST web services, ADF continues to serve as the centerpiece of the application architecture at many Oracle customers.

Oracle is also sharing their experience building the Oracle Cloud Applications with ADF through the Oracle Applications User Experience team. If you are building ADF applications, you can find user experience design patterns and beautiful, user-friendly sample applications with full source code at www.oracle.com/usableapps. I encourage you to visit.

I would also like to thank Oracle ACE Michael Rosenblum for the discussion over dinner overlooking the San Francisco Bay that led to this ADF Survival Guide, Jonathan Gennick from Apress for believing in the idea, Jill Balzano from Apress for shepherding the project to completion, and Oracle ACE Director Luc Bors for his many invaluable review comments.

Finally, I thank my wonderful wife for her love and support, and for accepting yet another batch of weekends marked "Book deadline" in our calendar.

Introduction

This book introduces you to Oracle ADF, which is used by many Oracle customers. ADF is a highly productive tool and is used to efficiently build user-friendly enterprise applications. Some of these ADF applications are new, some are replacements for legacy technologies like Oracle Forms, and some are extensions to Oracle's suite of Software-as-a-Service applications.

ADF developers are in high demand, and this book contains all the information you need to become a competent ADF developer.

In Chapter 1, you learn about building ADF applications using the declarative tools in JDeveloper. The power of ADF allows you to deliver a lot of bug-free functionality without having to write any code.

Chapter 2 explains ADF architecture and how to use ADF features to construct maintainable applications of all sizes.

In Chapter 3, you learn how to control the visual appearance of your application, and how to achieve the exact layout you want.

Chapters 4 and 5 explain how to add business logic to your application, both in the business component layer and the user interface layer.

In Chapter 6, you learn how to use ADF logging and debugging, and chapter 7 rounds off the book with a look at how to establish an efficient ADF development workflow.

CHAPTER 1

■ ■ ■

Drag-and-Drop Building

The secret behind the very high productivity that Oracle Application Development Framework (ADF) offers is the ability to build a lot of functionality without writing code. When building ADF applications, you should aim to write as little code as possible, using JDeveloper to drag and drop together the initial version of every page in your application.

This chapter explains how to use the ADF Business Component wizards and the graphical task flow builder, and how to build pages with automatic data binding.

Anatomy of an ADF Application

Oracle started out as a database company, and this heritage shines through in most of their development tools. Tools like Oracle Forms, Oracle Application Express (APEX), and Oracle ADF all start from the assumption that you already have a well-designed relational database with all the tables you need to store your data.

Above the database, an ADF application has two layers: the *business services layer* and the *user interface layer*. Between these two layers you find the *binding layer* that defines how the user interface layer is connected to the business services layer. Figure 1-1 shows the ADF high-level architecture.

© Sten Vesterli 2017
S. Vesterli, *Oracle ADF Survival Guide*, DOI 10.1007/978-1-4842-2820-3_1

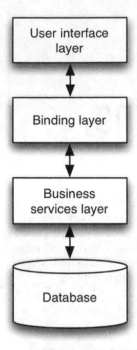

Figure 1-1. *ADF high-level architecture*

Business Services Layer

The business services layer provides the main functionality of the application. This includes all kinds of calculations, business rules, and the very important functionality of storing data. Behind the business service layer might be other technologies—there will typically be a relational database to store data, but your ADF application could also be purely based on web services. In this book, we will discuss ADF applications where the business services layer consists of ADF business components based on Oracle database tables. This is by far the most common way of building ADF applications and the approach recommended by Oracle.

User Interface Layer

The user interface layer contains the web pages your users will use to interact with your application. Building the user interface layer involves

- Deciding which pages your application is going to have

- Defining the navigation flow between pages

- Designing the actual pages with fields, buttons, and other user interface components

Binding Layer

The binding layer connects the user interface layer to the business services layer and is the secret sauce of Oracle ADF. When you create your application using the drag-and-drop functionality in JDeveloper, the binding layer is automatically created for you. It is thus possible to build perfectly functioning ADF applications without ever visiting the binding layer. But because a basic understanding of the binding layer is very useful in real-life ADF application development, we'll discuss it briefly at the end of this chapter.

Creating ADF Workspaces

An enterprise ADF application consists of many workspaces that each produce part of the overall application. When you work with ADF, you create your workspaces using *File ➤ New ➤ Application* and choosing the type *ADF Fusion Web Application* in JDeveloper. When you create such a workspace, JDeveloper will automatically create two projects inside the workspace:

- A model project for business components

- A view/controller project for the user interface

JDeveloper also automatically adds the right ADF libraries to each project and defines a dependency between them, so the view/controller project has access to the business components created in the model project.

JDeveloper calls a workspace an "application." This is a poor choice of word, because all but the very simplest ADF applications will involve more than one workspace.

Database Business Components

As mentioned in the introduction, Oracle ADF applications are normally built on top of a relational database. Oracle JDeveloper offers several wizards that make it easy to build all the types of ADF business components you will need in your business services layer. There are five main types of business components:

- **Entity Objects:** These objects correspond directly to tables, so there will be one entity object for every table your application uses. The entity objects handle the technical details of converting attribute value changes to INSERT, UPDATE, and DELETE statements sent to the database.

- **Associations:** These objects define relationships between entity objects and correspond to foreign key relationships in the database. The JDeveloper wizard normally automatically detects foreign key and creates matching associations, but you can also create them manually.

- **View Objects:** These objects define the specific data you need for a particular use case. A view object can use data from multiple entity objects and thus from multiple tables. For example, an *Employees* view object might show a department name from the *Departments* entity object in addition to the employee information from the *Employees* entity object.

- **View Links:** These objects represent master-detail relationships between view objects and allow ADF to coordinate the detail records with the master. For example, if you show a department with a list of its employees, the view link connecting your Departments view object with your Employees view object ensures that the Employees view object only shows records for that department.

- **Application Modules:** These objects collect instances of all the view objects used in an application or a subsystem. Application modules control the database transactions, allowing you to make changes in many different view objects in the application module and them commit or roll back all the changes in one transaction.

The different ADF business components can be visualized as shown in Figure 1-2.

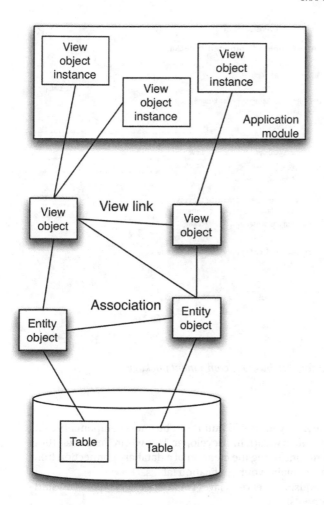

Figure 1-2. *ADF business components*

Keeping Organized

Your ADF application is going to contain a lot of business components of all five types. To make it easier for you to keep them separate so you can find the one you want, JDeveloper offers a preference setting that you should set.

In the JDeveloper preferences dialog under the ADF Business Components node, change the package prefix setting for each type. This setting means that every time a JDeveloper wizard creates a business component for you, it will automatically place it in an appropriately named subpackage under the root package of your business component project.

I recommend the settings shown in Figure 1-3.

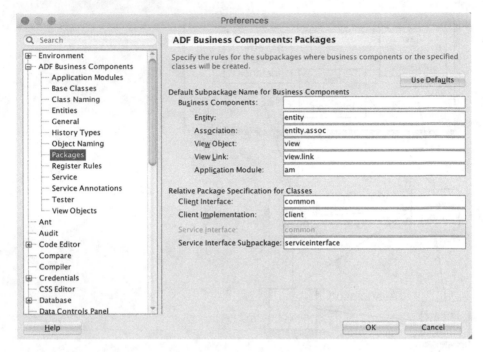

Figure 1-3. *Preference settings for ADF business component packages*

The Demo Wizard

When you start out with Oracle ADF, you should build your business components using the *Business Components from Tables* wizard in JDeveloper. This wizard initializes the project for business components, including the creation of a database connection from JDeveloper to the database that contains your application tables.

Make sure you select your business services layer (model) project before you start creating ADF Business components.

■ **Tip**   Decide on a database connection name early in the project and have everybody use that same name. When you combine your master application from multiple subsystems, it is much easier if everybody uses the same datasource name.

It takes you through up to six steps and optionally shows a summary.

1. Create entity objects. You can query the database connection and select the tables you want to create entity objects for. The wizard automatically creates associations for all foreign keys in the database between the selected tables.

2. Create entity-based view objects. A default view object is created for each entity object you select. It will contain all attributes from the entity object.

3. Create query-based view objects. This step allows you to create additional view objects based directly on SQL queries and not entity objects. These will not be updatable.

4. Create an application module and add an instance of all view objects in all possible combinations.

5. Create any REST web services. You'll need to define an initial version of the REST API to your business components and then select the view object you want to expose as REST web services.

6. Define which attributes you want included in each REST web service.

You can end the wizard at any time after the first step by clicking *Finish*.

Running the wizard and selecting the EMPLOYEES and DEPARTMENTS tables from the normal Oracle HR demo schema creates the business components shown in Figure 1-4.

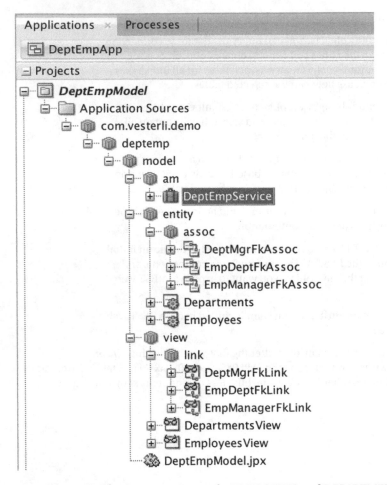

Figure 1-4. ADF business components for EMPLOYEES and DEPARTMENTS

Testing Business Components

Because an ADF application consists of both a business services layer and a user interface layer, it can be hard to debug problems by just running the application and interacting with the user interface. You can't tell if you should look for the problem in the business services layer or the user interface layer.

To address this challenge, JDeveloper offers the *Oracle ADF Model Tester*. This small application can be started from within JDeveloper by right-clicking an application module and selecting *Run*. When you do that, the Oracle ADF Model Tester application starts, loads the application module you clicked, and presents all the view object instances inside the application module. You can click each view object to see the actual data in the database with all business component logic applied. The ADF Model Tester application looks as shown in Figure 1-5.

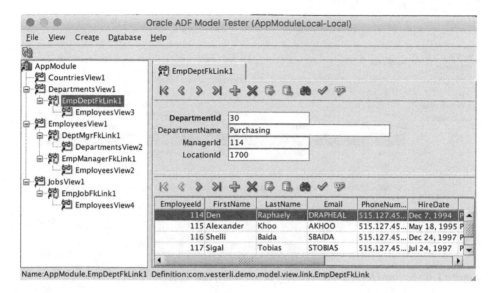

Figure 1-5. *ADF Model Tester*

You should always perform a simple test of your ADF business components with this little application to verify that your selection, validation, and business logic work the way you expect.

Entity Objects

Entity Objects correspond directly to database tables and handle object/relational mapping and data validation logic. There should be exactly one entity object for every database table, which allows you to implement business rules and validations in one place and be sure that it will always be applied.

By default, the JDeveloper wizards that create entity objects will create one attribute for every column in the corresponding table. There is no performance penalty involved in having every column represented as an attribute, because ADF will automatically perform optimizations to only query the attributes/columns that are relevant in any given situation.

Building Entity Objects

Because entity objects correspond directly to tables, there are few decisions to make when creating entity objects. You can use the *Business Components from Tables* wizard to create your initial entity objects—just don't select to create any view objects or application module.

When you have created your entity objects, you should open each of them and define the default label for each attribute that will be displayed to the user. You do this on the *Attributes* tab under the *UI Hints* subtab, as shown in Figure 1-6.

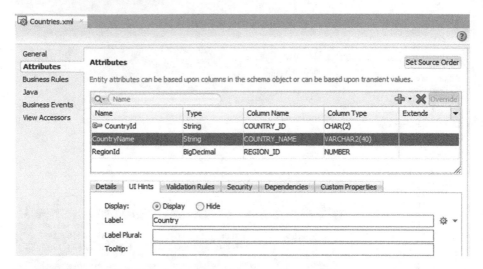

Figure 1-6. *Setting UI Hints for an entity object attribute*

The *Label* property and other elements on the *UI Hints* subtab will become the default values used in the user interface components showing that attribute. If you don't specify anything here, the attribute name (derived from the underlying database column) becomes the default label. The values provided at the entity object level can be overridden in each view object based on the entity object.

You might have a database trigger that creates primary key values for new records in the database. To tell ADF this, you need to change the type of your primary key attribute to the special *DBSequence* type. Open the entity object and then open the primary key attribute on the *Attributes* tab. When you change the *Type* field on the *Details* tab, several other settings change, including the *Refresh on Insert* setting. Together, these changes mean that your ADF application accepts that you don't enter a primary key value when creating a new record, and that ADF will ask the database to return the new primary key value when issuing an INSERT statement.

Building Associations

If you build all your entity objects in one pass through the *Business Components from Tables* wizard, the wizard should automatically create associations for all foreign key relationships in the database. If you don't create all entity objects at the same time, JDeveloper might not create the associations. In this case, you can create associations manually from JDeveloper. This is also necessary if your database for some reason does not contain foreign keys.

To get the maximum benefit from the JDeveloper wizards, you should make sure that JDeveloper knows about the relations in your data model.

View Objects

Where entity objects are oriented toward the database, view objects are oriented toward the user. Each view object represents a specific set of data collected for a specific need. Your user interface defines the view objects you need, including which attributes must be included.

Building View Objects

Because each view object is built for a specific purpose, you can't simply run a wizard and build a whole stack of them like you can with entity objects. Instead, you build view objects individually using the view object wizard in JDeveloper.

When running the wizard, you first select an entity object that will serve as the base entity object for the view object. By default, that entity object will be marked as updatable.

If you need additional data from other entity objects, you add those after adding the first. By default, these entity objects will be marked as *Reference* objects in JDeveloper. In Figure 1-7, the *Employees* entity object is selected first and is updatable. The *Departments* entity object is added later to get access to the department name.

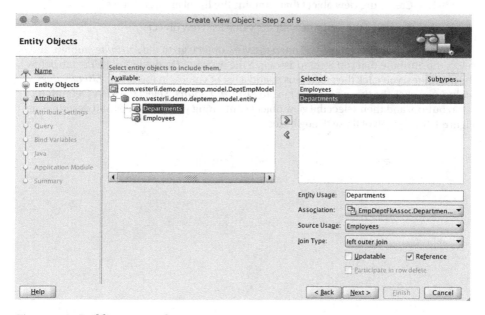

Figure 1-7. *Building a view object*

You can see from the figure that JDeveloper has figured out the connection between the two entity objects and refers to the corresponding association. If there were no association between the Employees and Departments entity objects, JDeveloper would have no way of connecting them.

The ordering of records is also defined as part of the view object definition (step 5, Query).

View object attributes also has a *UI Hints* subtab on the *Attributes* tab, just like entity objects do. This allows you to specify a default label, tool tip, and other user interface elements. If you don't specify anything here, the UI hints from the entity objects are used. If no UI hints were set at the entity object either, the attribute name (derived from the underlying database column) becomes the label.

Defining Lists of Values

In the places in your application where you want to limit the value of some attribute to a certain set, you normally define a code column with a foreign key to a table of allowed values. In the user interface, this is typically implemented with a drop-down list. This kind of relation is modeled in the view object in Oracle ADF, that is, in the business services layer. When you later use the view object on a page in your application, you can select how to represent this list of allowed values (various list components, radio groups, or other options).

There are two things to do to define a list of values like this:

1. Create the view object that contains the list of allowed values

2. Associate the attribute with the value list view object

To create this association, you open the view object, go to the *Attributes* subtab, and select the attribute that you want to associate the list with. On the *List of Values* tab below the attributes, you click the green plus to add a list of values. In the *Create List of Values* dialog, you click the green plus sign next to *List Data Source*, select the View Definition radio button, and then select the view object containing your list values and descriptions. Figure 1-8 shows all of these dialog boxes.

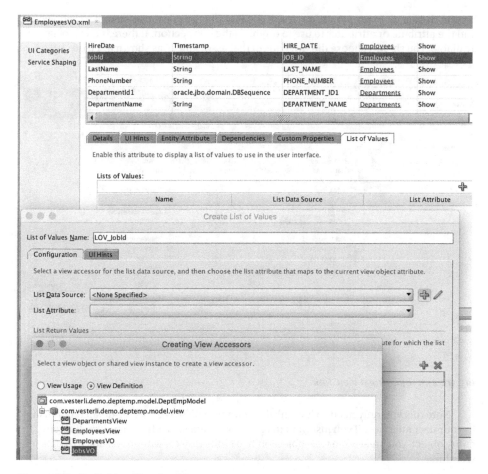

Figure 1-8. *Defining a list of values*

Don't overlook the *UI Hints* tab of the *Create List of Values* dialog. This is where you define which value is displayed to the user.

If you have a small number of values that you do not expect to change, you can create a static view object by setting the *Data Source* to *Static List* in the first step of the *Create View Object* wizard.

Building View Links

When your user interface contains a master-detail relation, like orders and order lines, or departments with their employees, you need a view link.

These are created manually with a JDeveloper wizard once you have created both the master and the detail view objects. Normally, a view link will be underpinned by an association between the main entity object behind the master and the main entity object behind the detail. In the view link wizard, you identify the master and detail view objects and the attribute or attributes to use to establish the connection. If there is an association available, you should choose the two ends of that association, as shown in Figure 1-9.

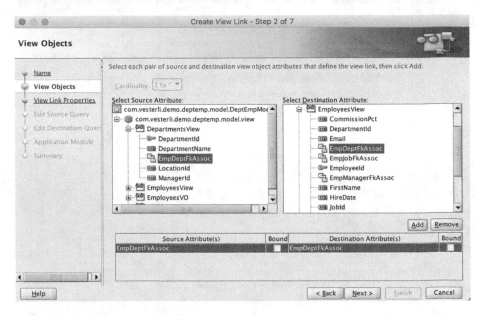

Figure 1-9. *Building a view link*

Note that you only need a view link if you want to display a master-detail relationship in your user interface. If you just want to enrich one data set with data from a different entity object, you create one view object on two entity objects without having to create a view link.

Creating View Criteria

A view object always contains the same attributes and the same sort order (unless you programmatically change it), but it doesn't have to always return the same records. To limit which records are returned by a view object, you can add *view criteria* and *bind variables*. If you are familiar with SQL, you can consider a view criterion as a named, declarative WHERE clause.

You add view criteria on the *View Criteria* tab in a view object. In the *Create View Criteria* dialog, you give your criteria a name and can add multiple criteria connected with AND or OR. Each criterion compares an individual attribute with either a literal value you hard-wire into the view criteria, or a bind variable you can create in this dialog. Figure 1-10 shows a view criterion.

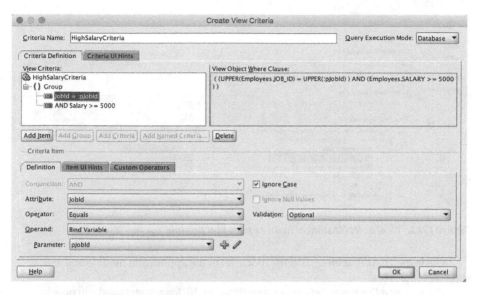

Figure 1-10. *Defining a view criterion*

When you have created a view criterion, you can use it when you add a view object instance to an application module. You can also programmatically apply it to a view object—we'll get back to that in Chapter 5.

Building Application Modules

The last ADF business component is the application module. These objects collect a number of view object instances that will be used in your application or subsystem. The application module controls the database transaction, allowing the user to make changes to many different view objects through many different screens and then committing everything to the database as one transaction.

Each view object instance is based on a view object, but one view object can be used in multiple view object instances in an application module. For example, Figure 1-11 shows an application module that contains three different instances of the EmployeeView view object.

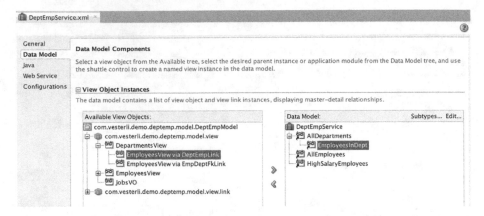

Figure 1-11. *View object instances in an application module*

The instance *AllEmployees* is at the root level of the application module and will show all employees.

The instance *EmployeesInDept* is subordinate to *AllDepartments* and will only show the employees in that department. To create one of these subordinate view object instances, you add the view object via a view link. In the figure, the *EmployeesInDept* instance is created by selecting *AllDepartments* to the right and selecting *EmployeesView via DeptEmptLink* to the left.

The instance *HighSalaryEmployees* is also a root-level instance on *EmployeesView*, but in this case, a view criterion has been applied to it. You can apply a view criterion by selecting the view object instance and then clicking the *Edit* button at the top right. This brings up the *Edit View Instance* dialog where you can set bind variables and apply view criteria.

Graphical Navigation Flow Design

When you have built the business services you need for your application, you need to create the user interface layer. You build this layer in three steps:

1. Partition your application into separate navigation flows.

2. Design each navigation flow.

3. Build the pages inside each navigation flow.

This section describes how to partition your application and design the navigation flows; building the actual pages is covered later in the chapter.

Partitioning Your Applications

All enterprise ADF applications will contain many separate navigation flows that each define how the user navigates between pages. Because Oracle developed ADF for their own very large applications (like Oracle Fusion Applications, a full ERP suite), modularity is central to ADF development.

The first step in developing the user interface of an ADF application is therefore to decide on which navigation flows you need. Your requirements normally serve as a good starting point, with each use case or user story a candidate to become a separate navigation flow.

Bounded and Unbounded Task Flows

The navigation flows you build in ADF are called *task flows* or sometimes *page flows*. ADF task flows are modular, and you can include one task flow in another. This allows you to build and maintain your entire application as a number of separate, reusable task flows that are combined into an application. We'll return to the architecture of the entire application in the next chapter.

Task flows contain actual pages or page fragments displayed to the user and control flows that define how the user is allowed to navigate between pages or fragments. It can also contain flow logic (branching) and can call business logic.

There are two types of task flows in ADF:

- Unbounded task flows
- Bounded task flows

Unbounded Task Flows

An unbounded task flow consists of a number of pages, and the user can start the task flow from any of these pages. There is thus not a strict boundary around the task flow.

Because every ADF view/controller project always has an unbounded task flow called adfc-config, you normally don't need to create these yourself.

An unbounded task flow is normally only used for first layer of navigation in the application. Many ADF applications have only one page in their unbounded task flow and then use various bounded task flows to expose the functionality of the application. How to swap different bounded contexts in and out will be discussed in Chapter 4.

Bounded Task Flows

A bounded task flow normally consists of a number of page fragments. It has a single well-defined entry point, one or more pages, and one or more exit points. Most of your application functionality will normally be implemented in the form of bounded task flows with page fragments.

You build your bounded task flows with page fragments in order to be able to reuse them. A page fragment should contain only the user interface elements necessary to perform the task it is designed for. It should not contain any common information like a header bar, logo, or menu. In this way, the task flow can be used and reused all over your application or even in different applications.

Because a page fragment is not runnable in itself, you need to embed it in a page in order to run it.

Creating Task Flows

The most common ADF architecture consists of one unbounded task flow and a number of bounded task flows using page fragments. Since you automatically get an unbounded task flow with every ADF Faces project, you will normally only need to create bounded task flows using page fragments. Because your task flows are part of the user interface layer of your application, make sure to select the view project in your workspace before you start creating task flows.

You find task flows in the *New Gallery* under *Web Tier* ➤ *JSF/Facelets*. In the *Create Task Flow* dialog, make sure you check both the *Create as Bounded Task Flow* and *Create with Page Fragments* check boxes, as shown in Figure 1-12. In a real-life enterprise application, you should use a template. We'll discuss templates in Chapter 2.

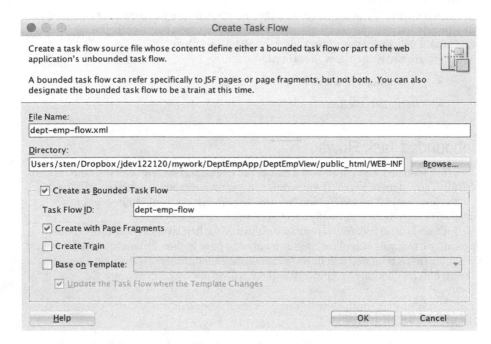

Figure 1-12. *Creating a bounded task flow with fragments*

When you have created a task flow, you are presented with a blank diagram with an instruction text in the middle.

Adding View Components

From here, you drag in *View* components from the *Components* palette (normally to the right). You need one view component for each page or page fragment you want in your application.

Note that the first view component you create automatically acquires a green "halo" behind it, indicating that it is the entry point of the bounded task flow. If you want another activity to be the entry point, you can right-click the icon for the activity you want invoked first and choose *Mark Activity* ➤ *Default Activity*.

Note that the view activities you add here are initially only placeholders. The actual page or page fragment is not created until you double-click a view activity. If you look carefully at the view activity icon, you can see that the bottom of the outline of the initial icons is a dashed line. Once you have created the page or page fragment, the icon changes to one with a solid outline all the way around.

Adding a Return Activity

Every bounded task flow should have at least one task flow return activity (the gray angle arrow). That indicates the exit point, that is, the point where control returns to any task flow that called this one. If you don't have a return activity, you won't be able to call the bounded task flow from another task flow because there is no way to return. Note that the return activity has an *outcome* property that you can set. If you have multiple task flow return activities, you can indicate to a caller what happened inside the flow—for example, you might have a return with success and another with error.

Adding Control Flow

When you have your view activities and the return activity, you add control flow cases (arrows) to define the navigation allowed between them. You can (and should) give each control flow case a short name. When you build your page and add a command component like a button, the various flows away from a page fragment will be offered as options. Figure 1-13 shows what a task flow might look like with a few view activities, a return activity, and some control flows.

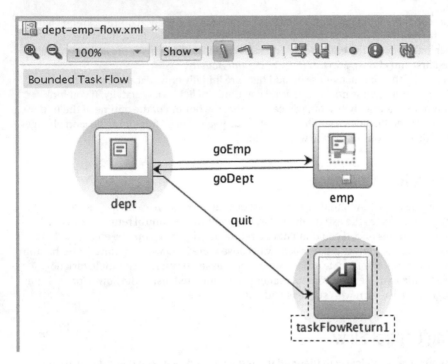

Figure 1-13. *A task flow*

If you want, you can also add *Router* activities. These allow the flow to process to different control flow cases based on the evaluation of an expression written in *expression language* (EL). We'll get back to that in Chapter 4, where we will also discuss how to drop in code elements from your business components.

Drag-and-Drop Pages

When you have created placeholders for your pages in the task flow design, it is time to create the corresponding page fragments. To do so, you double-click a view activity in a bounded task flow with fragments to open the *Create ADF Page Fragment* dialog.

Page Layout

In the Create ADF Page Fragment dialog, you have three options:

- Create Blank Page
- Reference ADF Template
- Copy Quick Start Layout

While learning ADF, use the *Copy Quick Start Layout* option. This allows you to select an example from a visual directory, as shown in Figure 1-14. When you make a selection, JDeveloper will add the corresponding layout components to your page fragment.

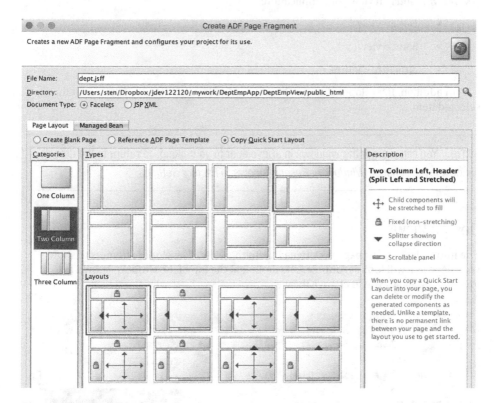

Figure 1-14. *ADF Quick Start Layouts*

In a real-life enterprise ADF application, you want to base all your pages and page fragments on page templates. We'll return to page templates in the next chapter.

Note that your page fragment should not contain decorative elements like a logo or a page header bar. If you need these elements in your application, they should be added to the master page that serves as the frame around your page fragment task flows. Page fragments often just have a one-column stretched layout in order to make use of all the available screen area.

Viewing Your Page

When you have created your page, it opens in the JDeveloper main window. There are several ways you can view your application:

- Design view

- Source view

- *Structure* window

In addition, JDeveloper shows a *Properties* window with details of the currently selected item.

■ **Tip**　You can reorder the windows in JDeveloper to your liking. To return to the default window layout, choose *Window ➤ Reset Windows to Factory Settings*.

Design View

The initial view of your page is *Design view*. In this view, JDeveloper attempts to show your page as it will look at runtime. The toolbar at the top of the window, shown in Figure 1-15, allows you to change the view.

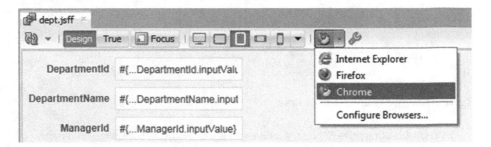

Figure 1-15.　*Design view*

The *Design* setting shows technical details about your page that can be useful when building the page: for example, the borders of layout components and technical details about the fields and their values. The *True* setting shows your page as it will look at runtime, with dummy data of the right data type (text, number, date). The *Focus* button shows only one layout container, which can be useful when you have a complicated layout with many nested containers. The different screen icons allow you to test your layout in various sizes and orientations (desktop, tablet horizontal, tablet vertical, smartphone horizontal, smartphone vertical). You can customize exactly how many pixels each size should represent. Finally, you can view your page or page fragment with dummy data in the various browsers you configure.

Source View

To see the actual source behind your page, you can change to the *Source view* by clicking the *Source* tab at the bottom of the window. This view shows all components and settings and allows you to freely make any change.

All components of an ADF page are part of a hierarchy, and you can collapse and expand nodes with the + and – icons in the left margin. The toolbar at the top of the window allows you to enable *Block Coloring*, where each node gets its own color to make the structure clearer. You can also ask JDeveloper to reformat your code if you have made manual changes.

By default, JDeveloper will show the *Mini-Map* in the right margin, giving you a visual overview of your code. You can close it from the context menu in the map, and display it again from the context menu in the source code (*Source* ➤ *Show Mini-Map*).

The far-right margin shows a green square at the top if your code is valid. If there are errors, the block at the top turns red and, and you get red bars in the margin corresponding to the location of the errors. Similarly, orange color indicates warnings.

If you have errors or warnings, a *quick fix* icon will often appear in the left margin, offering you JDeveloper's best guess at how to fix the code.

If you want to see line numbers, you can right-click in the left margin and choose *Toggle Line Numbers* from the context menu.

To change back to the design view, click the *Design* tab at the bottom of the window.

Structure Window

The *Structure* window, shown in Figure 1-16, shows another view of the hierarchy of components on your page.

Figure 1-16. *The Structure window*

By default, this window is placed in the bottom left corner of JDeveloper. The selections you make in the *Source* view and the selection in the *Structure* window are kept in sync by JDeveloper, so you can click an element in the *Structure* window to quickly jump to that place in the page source code. The *Design* and *Source* views, the *Structure* window, and the *Properties* window are just different representations of your application, so if you make a change in the *Source* view, for example, it is immediately reflected in the *Structure* window.

Adding Data-Bound Components

In a simple ADF Fusion workspace with a model and a view/controller project, you will automatically find the *Data Control* created from your application module in the *Data Controls* pane in the *Applications* window, as shown in Figure 1-17.

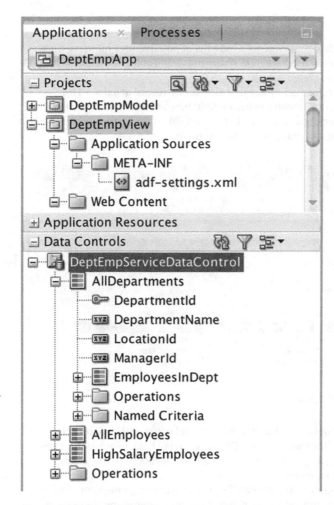

Figure 1-17. *Data Controls pane*

JDeveloper automatically creates one data control for every application module. Inside the data control, you can see all the view object instances in the corresponding application modules. From the Data Controls panel, you can, for example, drag a view object instance (the square red/orange icon, e.g., *AllDepartments*) or an individual attribute (the rectangular XYZ icon, e.g., *DepartmentName*) and drop it onto the page fragment.

When you drop an item from the data controls pane onto a page or page fragment, JDeveloper will automatically prompt you to select what type of user interface component you want to add. The list depends on the type of item, showing only those that are relevant to that item.

Adding a View Object Instance

When you drop a view object instance, you get a long list of possible user interface objects to create, but the most commonly used are *ADF Form* and *ADF Table* (ADF Table is found on a submenu under *Table/List View*).

If you select an ADF Form, you get a page that shows one record at a time. The attributes will be arranged vertically with a separate field for each attribute. You can check the *Row Navigation* check box, as shown in Figure 1-18, to ask JDeveloper to also add buttons to navigate to first, previous, next, and last record.

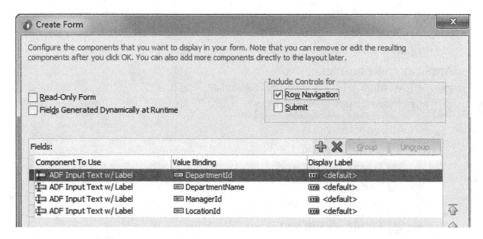

Figure 1-18. *Creating an ADF Form*

If you do not provide a label for each attribute, ADF will use the UI hint from the view object. If no UI hint was set in the view object, ADF will then fall back to any UI hint sent on the entity object. If no label is specified there either, the label becomes the attribute name derived from the database column.

Technically, JDeveloper creates an <af:PanelFormLayout> component containing individual <af:InputText> components connected to the attributes in the view object instance you drop. If you checked the *Row Navigation* check box, you also get buttons connected to the standard operations First, Previous, Next, and Last that every view object automatically offers.

If you select an ADF Table, you get a page that shows many records in a table with each record as one row in the table. You can select check boxes to enable sorting (by clicking the column header) and enable filtering (adding a filter criteria box at the top of each column). You can also specify each attribute label if you don't want to use the default. Technically, JDeveloper creates an <af:Table> component bound to the entire view object instance.

Adding an Individual Attribute

You can also drop an individual attribute onto a page or page fragment. In that case, your choices of user interface component are different—the most commonly used component is an *ADF Input Text w/ Label* that displays as a labeled input field as you'd expect. You can explicitly specify a label or accept the default coming from the view object UI hints, the entity object UI hints, or the database column name.

Adding an Operation

If you expand the Operations tab of a view object instance in the Data Controls pane, you will see a number of standard operations that ADF automatically provides for every view object. When dropping these onto a page or page fragment, you will be presented with a list of user interface components that make sense for an operation. The most commonly used are *ADF Button* and *ADF Link*.

In Chapter 5, you will learn how to add your own logic to view objects and application modules. The methods you add and decide to publish will also appear in the *Data Controls* pane and can easily be added to your application in the same way.

Adding Commit and Rollback

Just like the view objects, the application module also has an *Operations* tab at the very bottom in the *Data Control* panel (under all the view object instances). The two standard operations for an application module are *Commit* and *Rollback*. In order to perform a commit or rollback to the database, you simply need to drop one of these operations onto your page or page fragment. ADF will take care of everything for you, so you can build fully functional database applications without writing any code.

Implementing Navigation

You define the possible navigation between pages when you add control flow cases to your task flow. To actually implement the navigation in your user interface, you drop an action item (e.g., a button) onto your page. With the action item selected, open the *Properties* window, find the *Action* property, and choose from the list of options. You will see that this drop-down list contains all the control flow cases you have defined away from the current page.

When the user clicks the action item you have connected to the control flow case, your ADF application changes to that page.

■ **Tip** ADF handles temporary storage of values as the user navigates between pages. When the user eventually chooses a commit or rollback action, any changes will be committed to the database.

Examining Bindings

When you run an application you have built with these drag-and-drop features, data from your business components will automatically show up in the fields on your web pages. Changes made on the page are automatically propagated back to the business components, and if you commit, all the way to the database. The mechanism that connects business components to user interface elements is called *bindings*.

JDeveloper automatically creates them for you, and you can access them by clicking the *Bindings* tab at the bottom of your page. This produces a visual representation of the bindings that looks as shown in Figure 1-19.

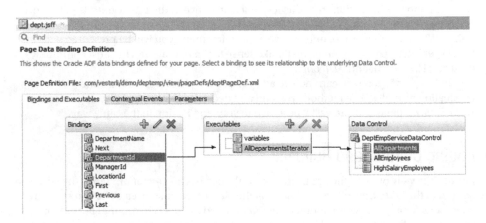

Figure 1-19. *Visual representation of bindings*

The *Bindings* column to the left shows the different bindings. The most commonly used are

- Attribute bindings (with the XY icon) for a single attribute.

- Tree bindings (with a folder hierarchy icon) for a whole view object instance.

- Action binding (with the gearwheel icon) for actions.

When you click a binding, an arrow appears pointing to an *Executable* in the middle column. This is most often an iterator that represents a pointer to a data collection in the data control shown in the right column.

There is a binding for each page, stored in a *page definition file*. To see the actual source code of the binding, you need to click the *Page Definition File* link at the top of the bindings window, or find the binding in the *Applications* window.

In many ADF applications, you won't need to change the bindings that JDeveloper creates for you. However, in advanced ADF applications, you might need to create a binding manually. You can click the green plus signs in the *Bindings* window to create both bindings and executables.

■ **Note** If you delete an element from a page or page fragment on the *Design* tab, JDeveloper tries to help you by automatically removing the corresponding binding. If you delete an element from the *Source* tab, JDeveloper assumes you are an advanced ADF developer and leaves the binding intact, so you can decide whether to keep it or manually delete it.

Minimum Viable Product

An enterprise ADF application normally consists of a number of bounded task flows using page fragments and a master page with a menu. When the user selects another menu item, the corresponding task flow is shown in a dynamic region on the master page. Because this way of building applications requires a bit of code, we'll return to it in Chapter 4.

However, you can build a fully functional application without any code. This allows you to present a running prototype to your users quickly and gather initial feedback.

A Simple Master Page

A basic master page can be built on the *One Column Header (Stretched)* Quick Start layout, as shown in Figure 1-20.

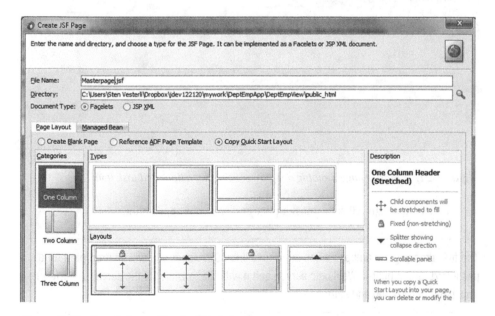

Figure 1-20. *One Column Header (Stretched)*

Inside that page, drop an *Output Text* component in the header area at the top and a *Panel Tabbed* component in the main area of the window. You find these in the *Components* window, by default in the right side of the JDeveloper window.

■ **Tip** You can use the search field at the top of the Components window to search for components by name.

In the *Create Panel Tabbed* dialog, create tabs for all the parts of your application you want to test.

Select your header text and use the *Properties* window to change the text, font style, and size.

Then drag your page flows onto the tabs of your application. When prompted for a user interface component, choose *Region*. We'll return to the other option (*Dynamic Region*) in Chapter 4. You will see the elements of your master page normally, and a grayed-out image of the first page of your task flow, as shown in Figure 1-21.

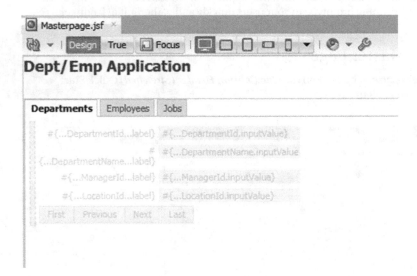

Figure 1-21. *A master page showing a region containing a bounded task flow*

You can now right-click the master page and run your application.

The first time you run an application after installing JDeveloper, you will be prompted for a password for the built-in WebLogic server, and it will take a while for the server to perform first-time initialization and startup.

You should see your task flows on the different tabs and be able to navigate between tabs.

Conclusion

You have now seen how to use the power of ADF and JDeveloper to build an entire, fully functional ADF application without writing a single line of code.

In the next chapter, we'll talk about how to build larger applications that make use of ADF's enterprise application development features, and in subsequent chapters you'll learn how to add Java code implementing business logic.

CHAPTER 2

ADF Enterprise Architecture

In the previous chapter, you saw how easy it is to build small, but fully functional ADF applications. This chapter will discuss how to build larger applications in an enterprise setting.

ADF Libraries

The secret behind ADF enterprise functionality is *ADF libraries*. An ADF library is like a normal Java Archive (JAR) file, but it contains extra metadata about its contents. This metadata allows JDeveloper to display the content and makes it easy to reuse components inside ADF libraries in JDeveloper.

Creating ADF Libraries

An ADF library is created from a project inside a workspace. When there are dependencies between projects in a workspace, the library will automatically include all objects from any projects it is dependent on. In a typical workspace of type *ADF Fusion Web Application*, JDeveloper automatically adds a dependency from the view/controller project to the model project. This means that when you create an ADF library from the view/controller project, you automatically get the content of the model project included in your library.

To create an ADF library from a project, you need a *deployment profile*. You create this by right-clicking the project and choosing *Deploy ➤ New Deployment Profile*. Choose an ADF Library JAR file type and give your profile a meaningful name. By convention, the profile name is of the format `adflibXxx` (e.g., `adflibHrDemoCommon`). The profile name becomes the default name of the ADF Library file.

■ Tip Because you might be handling ADF Library files outside JDeveloper (e.g., in your version control system or on application servers), the application name should be part of the library file name so you can tell the files apart.

© Sten Vesterli 2017

S. Vesterli, *Oracle ADF Survival Guide*, DOI 10.1007/978-1-4842-2820-3_2

In the Edit ADF Library JAR Deployment Profile Properties dialog shown in Figure 2-1, there is one setting you always need to change: *Connections*.

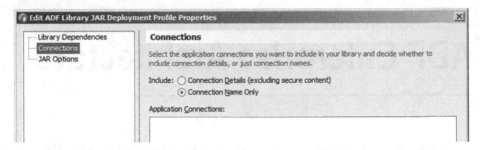

Figure 2-1. *Edit ADF Library JAR Deployment Profile Properties dialog*

The default option *Connection Details* means that your library will include the database connection details. You don't want your libraries to include the connection information to your local development database. Therefore, you need to select *Connection Name Only*. This means that your library will just include the *name* of your connection, not the technical details. It will then be up to your application server administrator to define a datasource with this name, pointing to the right database.

Managing ADF Libraries

Because ADF libraries are central to your development process, it is important that you manage them well. Each developer is free to release new ADF libraries at any time, but you need a review process before the libraries are shared to the whole team.

By default, ADF libraries are created in a `deploy` subdirectory within the project. You can leave them there and then tell your build/deployment manager when a new version is ready for wider distribution.

The build/deployment manager will then ensure that your ADF library file is tested and placed in the central location where everybody gets their ADF libraries. This approved version should be placed under version control.

Your process might be automated or manual, but you need an intermediate step that takes the ADF library built by some team, verifies it, and releases it for other teams to use.

Using ADF Libraries

To use an ADF library, you define a connection to the location in the file system where the approved libraries are stored, and add them to the project that needs them.

The connection is defined in the *Resources* window, by default to the right of the JDeveloper window. If you don't see it, you can open it from the *Window* menu. In this window, click the *New* icon at the top of the window and choose *IDE Connections* ➤ *File System*. Give your connection a name and select the path to the common ADF Library. The *Resources* window will now show all available libraries in that directory.

To use an ADF library in a project, select the project in the *Applications* window. Then right-click the library in the *Resources* window and choose *Add to Project*.

■ **Tip** If you want to see which ADF Libraries are included in a project, you can right-click the project and choose *Refresh ADF Library Dependencies…* This causes JDeveloper to reread all ADF libraries for the project and print them to the *Messages* window.

ADF Architecture Models

With the power of ADF libraries, you can create an ADF architecture that fits your need. There are many possibilities, but three good architectures are as follows:

- Simple
- Module
- Enterprise

Simple ADF Architecture

In a simple ADF architecture, you keep everything in one workspace. You will have a foundation project containing common code, a model project with your ADF business components, and a view/controller project with your task flows and master page.

This architecture works up to an application of no more than 20 task flows, implemented by a team of no more than three or four developers. If the application gets bigger than this, it becomes hard to find the component you need to work on, and JDeveloper gets slower as it must handle the interdependencies between more objects. If the team gets too big, members tend to get in each other's way, and there can be contention for central application files like DataBindings.cpx.

■ **Tip** To simplify your view of a large application workspace, check out the JDeveloper feature *Working Sets*, found under the *Working Set* icon (a funnel) at the top of the *Application* window. This feature allows you to limit what you see in JDeveloper.

Modular ADF Architecture

When building a single large ADF application, you should use a modular architecture. This involves several workspaces and projects, each worked on by a small team of one to four people.

There will be a foundation layer, a small number of subsystems, and a master application, as shown in Figure 2-2.

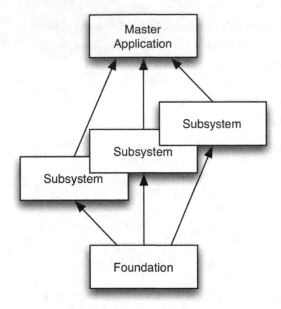

Figure 2-2. *Modular ADF architecture*

Foundation Layer

The foundation layer should be kept in one workspace with four projects:

- Common model

- Common UI

- Common utility code

- Business component base classes

When you create your foundation workspace, choose *ADF Fusion Web Application.* This wizard allows you to create the common model and common UI projects. Then add an extra project for utility and business component base classes with *File* ➤ *New* ➤ *Project* ➤ *ADF Model Project.* The reason you choose ADF model project is that this project template in JDeveloper already contains the technologies you need.

The common model project should contain all business components that can be shared across the entire application. Because entity objects map directly to database tables, these can be shared and go into the common model project. Similarly, view objects used for lists of values can also be shared and go into the common model.

The common UI project contains all shared elements that belong to the user interface layer. Elements in this project might include templates, skins, and declarative components.

The common utility code project contains any common utility classes that you will be using throughout your application.

■ **Tip**   Find the *Fusion Order Demo* application from Oracle and download it. This demo application contains several useful utility classes. Though not officially supported Oracle software, it can serve as a good starting point for your own utilities.

The business component base classes project contains your own ADF business component base classes that extend the Oracle-supplied classes. The section "Creating Your Own Base Classes" later in this chapter explains why you need these classes and how to build them.

Subsystems

The task flows that implement the functional requirements of the applications go into a small number of subsystems. Each subsystem should have its own workspace with a model and a view/controller project. A typical project will have three to eight subsystems, each assigned to a team of one or two developers.

The model project should contain the view objects that are specific to the use cases implemented by that subsystem.

The view/controller project should contain the bounded task flows that implement the use cases of the subsystem, together with their page fragments.

Master Application

The master application contains the master page with the global menu. All functionality is included in the master application through ADF libraries produced by the subsystems. Security is defined in the master application.

Enterprise ADF Architecture

If your organization has made a strategic choice of ADF as its development platform, you are likely to be building many ADF applications. In this case, it makes sense to establish an enterprise ADF architecture.

This involves an enterprise foundation layer common to all applications and an application foundation layer for each application. There will be a small number of subsystems and one or more master applications that utilize functionality from some of the subsystems. In an enterprise ADF architecture, some subsystems might be shared and used in several master applications. The architecture is illustrated in Figure 2-3.

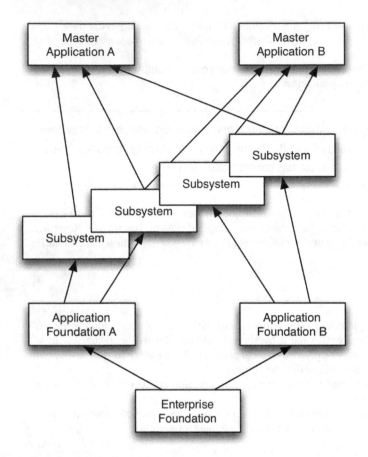

Figure 2-3. *Enterprise ADF architecture*

Enterprise Foundation

The enterprise foundation layer contains the code that is common across the entire enterprise. This layer should be kept in one workspace with at least two projects:

- Enterprise business component base classes

- Enterprise common utility code

As for the modular architecture, the business component base classes project contains extensions to Oracle's ADF business component base classes. At the enterprise level, you can add functionality that you want every ADF business component in the organization to have.

Similarly, the enterprise common utility code project contains utility classes that are expected to be used across all ADF applications in the organization.

Application Foundation

The application foundation layer contains application-specific code:

- Application-specific extensions to the enterprise business component base classes

- Application-specific common utility code

- Common model

The application-specific business component extensions extend the enterprise-level business component base classes and add any additional functionality only needed by this specific application. In the same way, the common utility code project contains common classes only useful in this application.

The common model project contains business components shared across the application as for the modular architecture (i.e., entity objects and a list of values view objects).

Subsystems

Subsystems in an ADF enterprise architecture are like subsystems in a modular architecture, and each consists of a model and a view/controller project.

Master Applications

Each master application is also like a master application in a modular architecture. In an ADF enterprise architecture, the same subsystem can be used in multiple master applications.

Deploying ADF Applications

Using these ADF architectures, your unit of granularity is the subsystem. If you make a change, you have to rebuild the subsystem ADF library and then build and deploy the master application EAR file.

If you want changes to your subsystems to take effect without needing to rebuild the master application, you can look at deploying your ADF libraries as *WebLogic shared libraries*, or investigate the ADF feature called *Remote Regions*.

Business Component Code

In the first chapter, you saw how you can build an Oracle ADF application without writing a single line of code. Of course, you are not limited by the ADF default business component functionality but can extend and customize it as you see fit.

Implicit Business Components

If you don't write any code yourself, you are *implicitly* using the ADF classes that Oracle delivers as part of the ADF framework. For example, whenever your application uses an entity object, ADF will automatically create an instance of the oracle.jbo.server. EntityObject class. That class reads the definition of your entity object (table, columns, and other settings) and provides a number of interfaces for the rest of the ADF Business component stack to call.

Explicit Business Components

You can create *explicit* business components on the *Java* tab for a business component by clicking the pencil icon in the top right corner of the tab. This brings up the *Select Java Options* dialog. The dialog is different for the different types of business components: Figure 2-4 shows what it looks like for an entity object.

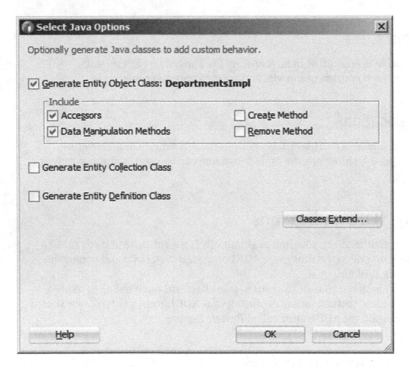

Figure 2-4. *Generating Java for an Entity Object*

If you do this, you will see that you get a Java class that extends the Oracle-supplied business component base class. Part of the code is shown in Listing 2-1.

Listing 2-1. Part of the Java for an Entity Object

```java
package com.vesterli.hrdemo.foundation.model.entity;
...
import oracle.jbo.server.EntityImpl;
...
// -----------------------------------------------------------------------
// ---     File generated by Oracle ADF Business Components Design Time.
// ---     Sat Feb 04 15:17:10 CET 2017
// ---     Custom code may be added to this class.
// ---     Warning: Do not modify method signatures of generated methods.
// -----------------------------------------------------------------------
public class DepartmentsImpl extends EntityImpl {
...
    /**
     * This is the default constructor (do not remove).
     */
...
    /**
     * Gets the attribute value for DepartmentName, using the alias name
       DepartmentName.
     * @return the value of DepartmentName
     */
    public String getDepartmentName() {
        return (String) getAttributeInternal(DEPARTMENTNAME);
    }
    /**
     * Sets <code>value</code> as the attribute value for DepartmentName.
     * @param value value to set the DepartmentName
     */
    public void setDepartmentName(String value) {
        setAttributeInternal(DEPARTMENTNAME, value);
    }
...
    /**
     * Add locking logic here.
     */
    public void lock() {
        super.lock();
    }

    /**
     * Custom DML update/insert/delete logic here.
     * @param operation the operation type
     * @param e the transaction event
     */
    protected void doDML(int operation, TransactionEvent e) {
        super.doDML(operation, e);
    }
}
```

41

You can see that your class is called `EntityImpl`. The import statement shows that this means `oracle.jbo.server.EntityImpl`. Depending on your choices in the *Select Java Options* dialog, JDeveloper will create some placeholder methods in the class where you can add your own code. For example, the *Data Manipulation Methods* check box has caused JDeveloper to create the `lock()` and `doDML()` methods.

You can always right-click anywhere in the code and choose *Source* ➤ *Override Methods* to ask JDeveloper to add a placeholder for any method in the Oracle-supplied base class.

As created by JDeveloper, these methods just invoke the corresponding method in the Oracle-supplied superclass. This means that generating Java for a business component does not change the functionality of the application until you add some of your own code.

Any changes you make to the specific business component (like `DepartmentsImpl` in this example) will only apply to that one business component. But you can also make changes that will apply to every business component in your application by creating your own ADF business component base classes.

Your Own Base Classes

You should always create your own ADF business component base classes, extending the Oracle-supplied classes. You don't have to add any functionality, but it is important that you create this extra layer of code so you have somewhere to place any common functionality you might desire in the future across all components. Figure 2-5 shows how your own base classes fit in between the Oracle-supplied classes and the specific business components used in your application.

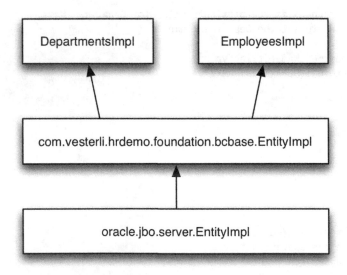

Figure 2-5. *Extending Oracle's business component base classes*

Creating Your Own Base Classes

Before you can create your own business component base classes in the BCBase project, you need to have JDeveloper load the ADF business component functionality. You do this by right-clicking the project and choosing *Project Properties*. Then choose *ADF Business Components* and check the check box *Initialize Project for Business Components*.

When you have done this, create your own base classes as standard Java classes (*File ➤ New ➤ Java Class*). There are 11 ADF business component base classes. You are only likely to ever add functionality to a few of these, but since it doesn't cost you anything to add your own base classes, and you never know when one of them might be useful in the future, you should create your own version of all of them. The Oracle classes, all of which can be found in the oracle.jbo.server package, are as follows:

- EntityCache

- EntityImpl

- ProgrammaticEntityImpl

- EntityDefImpl

- ViewObjectImpl

- ViewRowImpl

- ProgrammaticViewObjectImpl

- ProgrammaticViewRowImpl

- ViewDefImpl

- ApplicationModuleImpl

- ApplicationModuleDefImpl

For each of these, create your own version extending the relevant Oracle class, as shown in Figure 2-6.

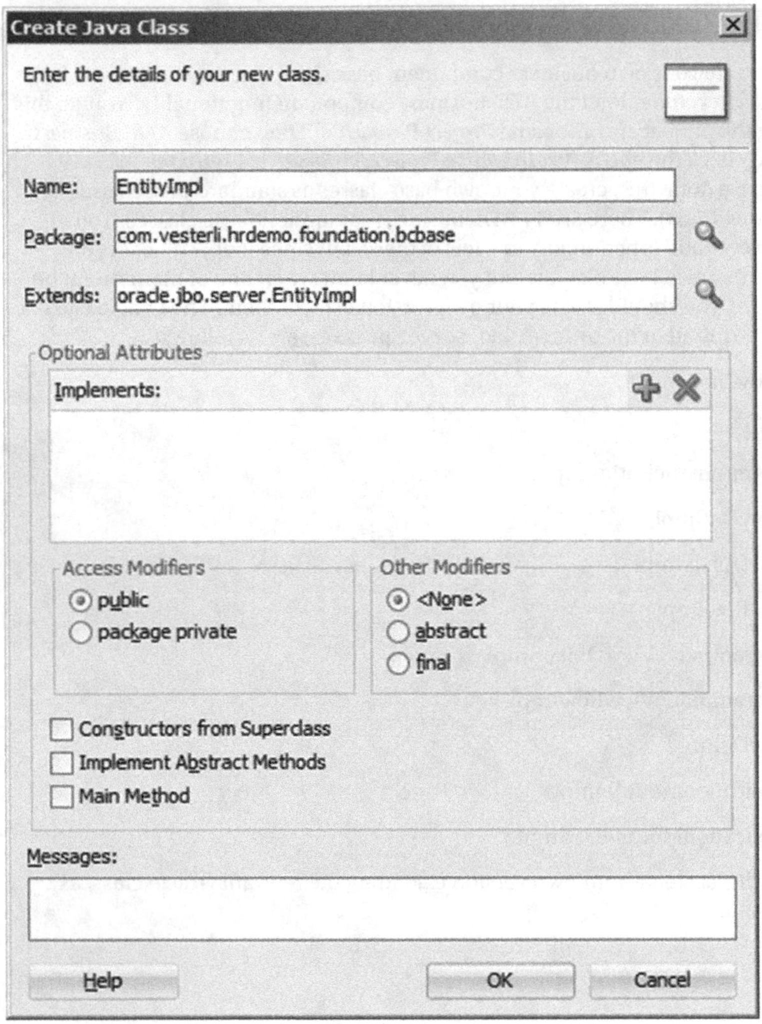

Create Java Class ☒

Enter the details of your new class.

Name: EntityImpl

Package: com.vesterli.hrdemo.foundation.bcbase 🔍

Extends: oracle.jbo.server.EntityImpl 🔍

Optional Attributes

Implements: ➕ ✖

Access Modifiers
- ⦿ public
- ⦾ package private

Other Modifiers
- ⦿ <None>
- ⦾ abstract
- ⦾ final

- ☐ Constructors from Superclass
- ☐ Implement Abstract Methods
- ☐ Main Method

Messages:

Help | OK | Cancel

Figure 2-6. *Creating your own business component base class*

Your code will look similar to Listing 2-2.

Listing 2-2. Code for Your Own Business Component Base Class

```
package com.vesterli.hrdemo.foundation.bcbase;

public class EntityImpl extends oracle.jbo.server.EntityImpl {
}
```

Note how simple this class is: it only has a name and the information that it extends the Oracle-supplied base class. This is all you need at the beginning of a project—you can add your own methods, overriding the method from the Oracle class as needed.

When done, create an ADF library from your BCBase project and place it in your common ADF library directory for everybody to use.

Using Your Own Base Classes

Once you have created your own ADF business component base classes, you can set up JDeveloper to always use them whenever creating new business components. You do this under JDeveloper preferences under *ADF Business Components* ➤ *Base Classes*. For every base class, replace `oracle.jbo.server` with the package that your base classes reside in, as shown in Figure 2-7.

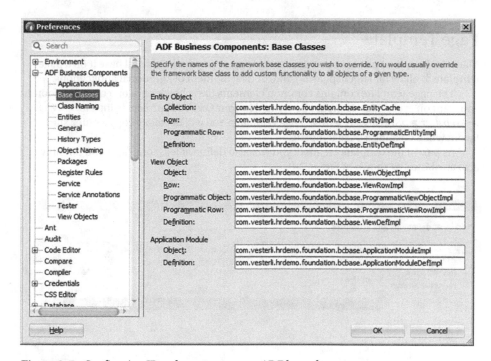

Figure 2-7. *Configuring JDeveloper to use your ADF base classes*

Making the change under JDeveloper preferences means that every business component created from now on will be based on these classes. This also means that your application will fail at runtime if the ADF library containing your ADF business component base classes is not added to the project.

If you want to change the base classes for an individual project, there is a similar setting under *Project Properties*.

Using Templates

As is to be expected from an enterprise development framework, Oracle ADF also offers various options to base your user interface elements on templates. If you create your pages, page fragments, and task flows on templates, you have the option to easily add or change things across your entire application or enterprise later. If you don't use templates, you must make any necessary global changes in each page, fragment, or task flow.

Since there is no cost involved in basing everything on templates except the need for a little thought up front, you should always use them. Even if you don't have any content to go into the templates at the start of the project, create empty templates and build your application on these.

All templates are created in a view/controller project in your foundation workspace. If you are using an enterprise architecture, both your enterprise foundation and your application foundation should have templates.

Page Template

Many ADF applications have just one master page, but you should still base it on a page template to allow for later expansion and/or development of additional applications.

The page template contains common elements like a header bar or a common footer you want on every page. It should be created in your CommonUI project using *File* ➤ *New* ➤ *Web Tier* ➤ *JSF/Facelets* ➤ *ADF Page Template*. You will normally copy a quick start layout when creating a page template.

As part of the template creation, you will also define at least one facet and possibly also attributes, as shown in Figure 2-8.

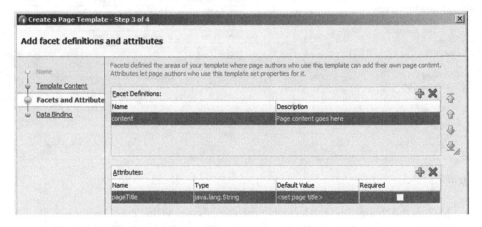

Figure 2-8. *Defining template facets and attributes*

Using Facets

A facet is a place where the user of the template can add his or her own content. A template normally has one facet, but there could be multiple if your layout requires two separate content areas.

When you have created the template, it is shown in the JDeveloper main window. Here, you add decorations like logos, headers, and so forth. All of the elements in the template will become part of every page based on the template.

In the place where you want the actual page content, you drop a *Facet Definition* (<af:facetRef>) from the *Components* palette. You will be prompted for a facet name, with the options being the facets you defined when creating the template.

Using Attributes

Often, you want to be able to change text placed in the template area. For example, your template might define a colored bar across the top of the page, and you want the page name to be written inside this bar. On the page based on the template, you can't add anything inside the template area. However, you *can* assign values to template attributes.

This is used as follows:

- When defining the template, create an attribute (e.g., pageTitle).

- In the template, place a text element (e.g., <af:outputText>) where you want the page name. Set the *Value* property of the text element to match the attribute (e.g., #{attrs.pageTitle}). Apply any style you want to the text element (font size, etc.).

- Create a page based on the template. In the *Source* view, select the <af:pageTemplate> element, find the field for the template attribute in the *Properties* window, and set it to the desired value.

Page Fragment Template

The body of your application will consist of page fragments in bounded task flows. Because these fragments will live inside a master page in your application, they do not normally contain any decoration like headers or footers.

Your page fragment template will therefore normally just consist of a one-column stretched layout to ensure that your fragment will make use of all available space on the page. Define one content facet and place the facet reference in the stretch layout.

■ **Note** It might seem superfluous to base page fragments on a template, but it doesn't cost anything to do, and it can save you from a lot of work in the rare cases where you do find the need to add something common to every page fragment.

Task Flow Template

You can also base your bounded task flows on a template. This allows you to add functionality later or to set properties globally across your entire application.

One reason to do this could be to add common initializers and finalizers to each task flow. These are pieces of code that ADF will automatically execute on entering and leaving a task flow, and they are often used for application performance tracking.

Like page fragment templates, you might not have an immediate need for task flow templates, but it doesn't cost you anything to create them. By basing all your application task flows on templates, you get the option to easily make some changes to every task flow.

Application Skin

The visual appearance of your application is determined in part by the *ADF Skin*. If you do not create one, an ADF default skin will be used.

Your own ADF skins are always based on one of the standard skins that are part of ADF, and everything that you do not explicitly change will have the default ADF look. This means that you can create an empty skin at the outset of your project and place it in the foundation workspace without affecting the look of the application.

If you base all your subsystems and the master application on this skin, you have again established one point to make application-wide changes.

We'll return to skins in Chapter 3.

Common Model

In an ADF application, you can also reuse some business components across subsystems. These reusable components should be placed in a common model project in the foundation workspace. Business components can typically only be reused within an application, so the enterprise foundation layer in an ADF enterprise architecture is unlikely to contain shared business components.

When you create the foundation workspace as an *ADF Fusion Web Application*, JDeveloper will automatically establish a dependency between the model (CommonModel) and the view/controller (CommonUI) project. You should remove this dependency in your foundation project (*Project Properties ➤ Dependencies*). The dependency means that when you create an ADF library from the view/controller project, everything in the model project is automatically included. That's fine for subsystems, but in the foundation, you want to explicitly deploy each project to an ADF library.

Sharing Entity Objects

Remember that entity objects map database tables to an object representation that can be used by view objects. This means that for every database table, you only need one entity object. Therefore, it makes sense to create all of them in a common model project that you deploy as an ADF library from a common model project in your foundation workspace.

Sharing List of Value View Objects

View objects contain attributes collected for a specific purpose. This means that they are generally built as part of a subsystem to implement the use cases or stories in that subsystem. However, every time you implement a value list for an attribute, you also need a view object. Many of these will be used in multiple subsystems, so it makes sense to place them in the common model project in the foundation together with the entity objects.

Your common model project also needs one application module. This allows you to run and test your list of value view objects, and the application module can also be used as a *shared application module*. Refer to the chapter *Sharing Application Module View Instances* in the Oracle manual *Developing Fusion Web Applications with Oracle Application Development Framework* for more on shared application modules.

Building Subsystems

The main body of an ADF application goes into the subsystems. Each subsystem should be created in a separate workspace with a model and a view/controller project.

Your subsystem workspace will make use of all the ADF libraries from the foundation layer: common UI, common model, business component base classes, and any common utility code.

In the model project, you create the view objects and view links that are needed to implement the stories or use cases of the subsystem. All of them should be based on entity objects that come from the common model.

■ **Tip**   If you don't see any entity objects when creating view objects, you probably did not add the dependency to the common model ADF library properly.

In the view/controller project, you create bounded task flows with page fragments, matching your use cases, stories, or UI wireframes. These should be based on the page flow template from the common UI ADF library.

After creating the task flows, you create the actual page fragments, based on your page fragment template.

Because you can't run task flows with page fragments directly, your subsystem normally also contains a test page for each task flow. You can also use the *ADF EMG Task Flow Tester*, which is a JDeveloper extension developed by members of the ADF Enterprise Methodology Group (ADF EMG). You install this useful tool like other JDeveloper extensions by selecting *Help ➤ Check for Updates*. Be sure to check the check box *Open Source and Partner Extensions* in the first step of the *Check for Updates* wizard. You should see this tool in step two of the wizard, as shown in Figure 2-9.

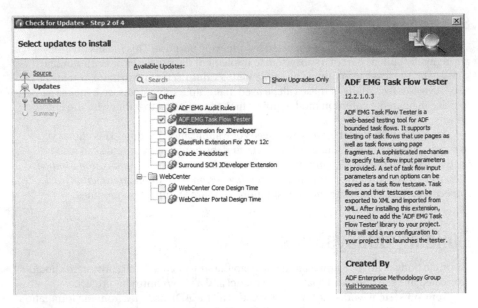

Figure 2-9. *Installing the ADF EMG Task Flow Tester*

Allow JDeveloper to restart and follow the instructions to start using the ADF EMG Task Flow Tester.

Building the Master Application

The master application is where all the subsystems come together. It has its own workspace and uses all the ADF libraries from the foundation level and all subsystems. In the master application workspace, you only use the view/controller project—all business components reside in a foundation layer or in a subsystem.

Master Application Content

The master application contains the master page (a page, not a fragment), based on the page template.

Since the page template contains any application decoration (header bar, logo, etc.), the page itself will only contain a menu, a dynamic region, and some code. The code handles swapping the content of the dynamic region to show another bounded task flow. We'll see an example of the necessary code in Chapter 5, where we discuss application logic.

Security

Finally, you apply security in the master application. To apply security, you select *Application* ➤ *Secure* ➤ *Configure ADF Security* and go through the *Configure ADF Security wizard.*

■ **Note**   ADF Security is available in ADF applications running on WebLogic and WebSphere application servers. If you are running the free *ADF Essentials* edition and deploying on GlassFish, you do not have access to ADF security. You can secure web pages through other means (e.g., Apache Shiro) but must write your own authorization code if you want to limit access at the task flow level.

Running the Configure ADF Security Wizard

In the first step, choose *ADF Authentication and Authorization* to ask ADF to handle both authentication (identifying the user) and authorization (what the user is allowed to do).

In the second step, choose *Form-Based Authentication* and check the check box *Generate Default Pages*. This creates basic login pages with all the necessary information and fields. You can then change them to match your application. *HTTP Basic* and *HTTP Digest* leave the login to the browser, presenting your user with whatever ugly dialog box their browser uses for authentication.

In the third step, chose *No Automatic Grants* to indicate that you will explicitly assign access rights.

In the fourth step, don't check the *Redirect Upon Successful Authentication* check box. You normally just want to show the master page to the user, not redirect to some other page.

When you finish the wizard, your application is secure and will prompt you for a username and password. It also won't allow you access to anything until you define access rights.

Defining Access Rights

Access rights are defined in the jazn-data.xml file created by the security wizard. You can choose *Application* ➤ *Secure* ➤ *Application Roles* to view this file in a user-friendly dialog instead of having to edit the file itself.

As an application developer, you create application roles for the different types of users in your application. Many applications have only one level of security where every authenticated user can use the full functionality of the application. In this case, you only need one application role. Other applications have several types of users and would need multiple application roles.

On the *Application Roles* tab of the jazn-data.xml file, you name these application roles. On the *Resource Grants* tab, you select resources and grant them to specific roles. If you have complicated security requirements, you might also use *entitlement grants*, which are groups of resources.

Typical ADF security uses the following grants:

- *Web Page* grant for the application master page to every application role.

- *Task Flow* grant for the different task flows to different application roles if necessary.

51

In an ADF application using the modular or enterprise architecture, the task flows are developed in subsystems and brought into the master application through ADF libraries. To grant access to these task flows, be sure to check the check box *Show task flows imported from ADF libraries*.

If you want to secure data sets, you can use *ADF Entity Object* grants. If you want to secure individual attributes, you use *ADF Entity Object Attribute* grants.

Running in the Built-in WebLogic

On the *Test Users & Roles* tab, you can define test users and assign roles to them. These users are only used when running the application in the built-in WebLogic server in JDeveloper.

You can assign the application roles defined in your application to individual test users or to groups of users (called *Enterprise Roles* in JDeveloper). This allows you simulate the authorization logic that will apply when deploying to a stand-alone application server.

Deploying to Test and Production Servers

When you deploy your application to stand-alone test and production servers, part of the deployment is to map application roles to the users or groups on the server.

In a typical enterprise setting, your WebLogic server will be integrated with some identity provider (e.g., Microsoft Active Directory). This means that when you assign application roles in Oracle Enterprise Manager Grid Control, you can see and assign to your AD users and groups.

For example, your application might have application roles readonly, normal, and superuser. In your identity management system, you might have groups of users called Trainee, Customer Service, and Senior advisor. When deploying the application, you could map readonly to Trainee, normal to Customer Service, and superuser to Senior advisor.

Conclusion

You've seen how ADF Libraries allows you to split the development of even very large enterprise applications into manageable pieces, and how to build all the foundation elements you need before you start building in earnest.

In the next chapter, we will discuss how to achieve the layout and appearance you want for your application.

CHAPTER 3

■ ■ ■

Layout and Skins

As you saw in Chapter 1, JDeveloper can produce acceptable layouts and visual appearance when building simple drag-and-drop ADF applications. This chapter will explain how to get more control over the layout and appearance of your ADF application.

For this, ADF offers the following functionality:

- Layout components

- Individual component styling

- Application-wide skinning

You use layout components like *Panel Grid Layout* to arrange components on your pages and page fragments. You can nest layout components within each other to achieve exactly the layout you want, and control the spacing between elements with Spacer components.

To change the look of an individual component, you change the *InlineStyle* property. ADF components are controlled with standard Cascading Style Sheet (CSS) formatting, and you can set an explicit style for one component or define a style class.

The look of every component in the entire application is controlled by the application skin. A skin consists of a CSS file, optionally supplemented with resource bundles to customize the default strings used in ADF applications, and possibly also your own image files. Your application is always based on a default skin, so you only need to change the things that you want to look different from the default.

Layout

Many years ago, the first technology for producing web pages with Java was JavaServer Pages (JSP). In JSP, presentation and business logic in Java code were mixed together with the HTML tags that defined the page shown to the user. This made for web pages that were very hard to maintain. Over time, developers learned to separate the Java code into tag libraries to try to clean up the mess, but using tag libraries right still required discipline from the developer.

JavaServer Faces (JSF) solves this problem once and for all. A JSF page consists only of components, and any presentation logic is placed in separate Java Bean classes. We'll return to presentation logic in Chapter 5. ADF is based on JSF, and ADF user interface components are special JSF components delivered by Oracle.

© Sten Vesterli 2017
S. Vesterli, *Oracle ADF Survival Guide*, DOI 10.1007/978-1-4842-2820-3_3

Some components like data input fields and drop-downs display data. Other components perform actions like performing navigation and invoking business logic. Finally, some components serve to arrange components on the page. These are the layout components that we will be discussing in this chapter.

Layout Managers vs. Fixed Formatting

In some development tools (e.g., Oracle Forms), you place components in a fixed position on the page. For example, you might place an input field at position x=150, y=220. This means that the component will always be placed 150 pixels in from the left margin, and 220 pixels below the top margin. This approach gives you full control but is also inflexible. If the user runs the application on a larger monitor, everything will stay as defined by the developer and the extra space goes unused.

In an ADF application, the layout is dynamic and can depend on the size of the browser window the application runs in. The layout is handled by *layout manager* components that arrange the components placed inside them. Layout managers can control other layout managers, leading to a whole hierarchy of layout managers. This allows you to create the exact layout you want.

Some layout components simply control other elements—for example, a panel grid layout control grid row components, and a tabbed panel controls detail items. Other layout components have *facets* that can hold other components. For example, a panel stretch layout has top, bottom, start, center, and end facets with specific locations. Components you drop in the top facet of a panel stretch layout will always be placed highest on the screen, and everything in the center facet will be below that.

■ **Note** Some components (like panel stretch layout) have *start* and *end* facets, not left and right. This is because ADF supports right-to-left languages like Arabic, Hebrew, or Persian. If you configure your application for one of these languages, the start facet moves to the right, because that is where reading starts.

Stretching and Nonstretching

When the layout managers arrange components on the screen, they take into account the stretching properties of each layout component. There are four types of ADF layout components:

- Those who can stretch themselves and stretch their children

- Those who don't stretch themselves, but do stretch their children

- Those who can stretch themselves, but don't stretch their children

- Those who don't stretch themselves and don't stretch their children

An ADF application normally starts with a stretchable outer layout container that stretches its children (like a *Panel Grid Layout* with a 100% height row and a 100% width cell). This makes sure that your application will use all available browser space.

Some components can't stretch (e.g., *Input Text*), so you should avoid placing these as direct children of a layout container that will attempt to stretch its children. Instead, you wrap your nonstretchable components in a layout component like *Panel Group Layout*, which stretches itself but doesn't stretch its children.

Quick Start Layouts

When learning about ADF layout, the best starting point is the *Quick Start Layouts*. These demonstrate best practice and evolve together with ADF. For example, in earlier versions of ADF, the outer layout container of the quick start layouts was a *Panel Stretch Layout*. However, when ADF got the improved *Panel Grid Layout* component in version 11.1.2, some of the quick start layouts changed to demonstrate the right way to use this new component.

When you create a page or page fragments, choose *Copy Quick Start Layout* and choose the example that most closely matches what you are trying to achieve. First, select the number of columns (one, two, or three) from the *Categories* panel to the left. Then, choose a type and finally a layout, as shown in Figure 3-1.

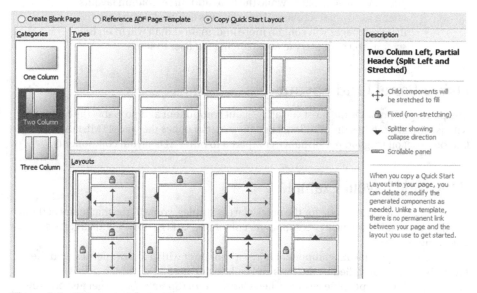

Figure 3-1. *Using a quick start layout*

In the layout selection, you will see a few different icons:

- The four-way arrow indicates an area that will stretch as much as possible. This is a good choice for the main work area of your page.

- The padlock indicates an area that will not change in size. JDeveloper only offers these fixed-size areas around the margins (top, left, bottom, and in a few cases, to the right). These areas are normally used for page headers, menus, and task lists that you know will take up only limited space.

- The triangle indicates that JDeveloper will use an `<af:panelSplitter>` component. This component is shown in the application as a line with a little triangle, and the user can click the triangle to collapse the area that the triangle points to. This is often used to create a place for supplementary information that the user might or might not need to see all the time.

- The scrollbar indicates that JDeveloper will use an `<af:panelGroupLayout>` with layout `scroll`. In the application, this layout will be shown with a scrollbar if there are more components than will fit on the page. The one-column layouts offer a vertical scrollbar while the two- and three-column layouts offer a horizontal scrollbar. These layouts are used if you know that your pages will contain more information than will fit on the screen. You should try to avoid forcing the user to scroll.

Using Panel Grid Layout

The panel grid layout is the most versatile layout component and probably the one you will use the most. It has the additional benefit that it matches the way HTML tables are laid out, so it offers good performance compared to other ADF layout components.

Panel Grid Layout Example

If you look at the source code for the quick start examples, you will see that many of them use an `<af:panelGridLayout>` component, containing `<af:gridRow>` and `<af:gridCell>` components.

The panel grid layout component is just a container with a few properties, and the layout is mainly controlled by the rows and cells inside it.

In the simplest possible layout, called *One Column (Stretched)*, you get just one row and one cell. The *height* property of the row is set to 100%, meaning the row will stretch to take up all vertical space. Inside the row, the cell has the *width* property set to 100%, meaning the cell will stretch to take up all horizontal space. The cell also has both the *halign* and *valign* properties set to *stretch*. This means that the cell will attempt to stretch components inside it. The net effect of these components and settings is a layout that will take up all available space in the browser window and use it for its content.

Creating Your Own Panel Grid Layout

You can also add a panel grid layout to a page from the *Components* window. This can be useful if you decide you want more detailed control over the layout of a part of the page. Experienced ADF developers also often just create their pages blank and add layout components themselves.

When you drop a panel grid layout component on a page, the Create Panel Grid Layout wizard appears as shown in Figure 3-2.

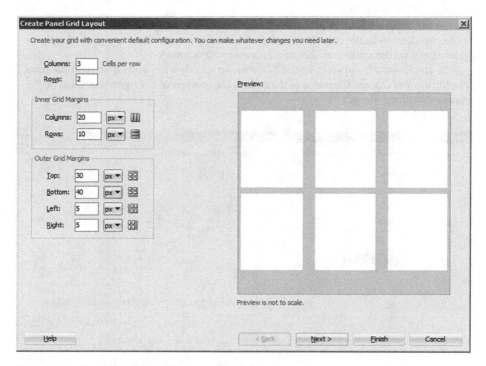

Figure 3-2. *Create Panel Grid Layout wizard*

You decide on the number of rows and columns and the margins. The inner grid margins define the spacing between rows and cells inside the grid, and the outer grid margins define the spacing between the edge of the panel grid layout and the outermost cells. For example, in the preceding figure, there are 30 pixels from the top of the grid layout to the first row, then 10 pixels between rows, and then 40 pixels between the last row and the bottom of the panel grid layout.

In the second step of the wizard, you can define the initial width and height of the cells and define if some cells should span several rows or columns.

The choice you make on the *Grid Width* tab is used as the *width* property of all cells in the column. By default, the JDeveloper wizard specifies width in percent, distributing space evenly between the columns.

■ **Tip**   Specify cell widths in percent and make sure the total adds up to 100%. If you mix units (pixels and percent, for instance) or don't allocate all space, the results are undefined.

You can also set the width to *auto* or *dontCare*. For a cell, *auto* width means it will be sized according to the components in the cell. The *dontCare* setting for a cell means that the other cells in the column can define the width. You probably don't want to set *dontCare* for a whole column, because this means ADF is free to give the column whatever width it feels like.

On the *Grid Height* tab, the row height is always *auto*, meaning the height is defined by the components in the row. After the wizard is complete, you can change the height to a percentage (of the space not already allocated to other rows).

On the *Spans* tab shown in Figure 3-3, you can specify if any cells span multiple rows or columns. You can see the name of the cells in the Preview to the right—they will be named something like gc1,3.

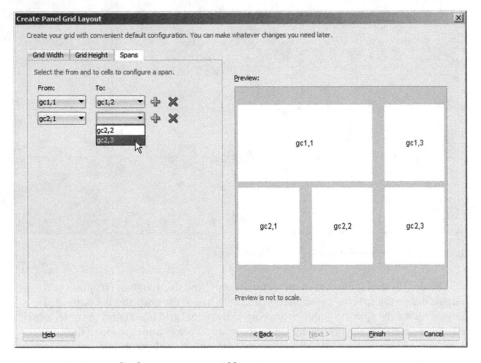

Figure 3-3. Row and column spans in grid layout

You define each span by defining the *From* grid cell (top, left) and the *To* grid cell (bottom, right). JDeveloper will try to show only the options that make sense in the second drop-down, but you can create impossible spans that don't make sense. In this case, the appearance in the application is, of course, undefined.

When you finish the wizard, JDeveloper creates an `<af:panelGridLayout>` tag and places the necessary `<af:gridRow>` and `<af:gridCell>` tags inside it with the relevant properties set. You can change the properties either in the Properties window or in the source view. Spans are controlled with the `columnSpan` and `rowSpan` properties: the value you set for these properties indicates how many cells you want to merge. This is similar to the way HTML `<td>` tag uses `colspan` and `rowspan` properties.

Using Panel Form Layout

A very common layout is having several input elements arranged below each other in one column. You can build this kind of layout with panel grid, but ADF has a specialized layout manager for this: the *Panel Form Layout* (`<af:panelFormLayout>`).

You create this layout by dragging a *Panel Form Layout* component onto your page from the *Components* window. When you drop a collection onto a page from the *Data Controls* pane as you saw in Chapter 1, JDeveloper will also use a panel form layout.

Inside the panel form layout, you can place the data components you need. Often, you will drag these in from the Data Controls panel as individual attributes in order to get JDeveloper to create the necessary data binding automatically.

The panel form layout contains a *footer* facet that is often used for buttons to navigate, save data, or execute business logic, typically placed inside a panel group layout. For example, the code you get when you drop a view object instance as an ADF Form and check the *Row Navigation* check box looks like Listing 3-1.

Listing 3-1. Example of Panel Form Layout

```
<af:panelFormLayout id="pfl1">
    <af:inputText ... />
    <af:inputText ... />
    <af:inputText ... />
    <f:facet name="footer">
        <af:panelGroupLayout layout="horizontal" id="pgl2">
            <af:button ... text="First" ... />
            <af:button ... text="Previous" ... />
            <af:button ... text="Next" ... />
            <af:button ... text="Last" ... />
        </af:panelGroupLayout>
    </f:facet>
</af:panelFormLayout>
```

The two most important properties controlling a panel form layout is the *MaxColumns* and *Rows* properties.

- *Rows* control how many input elements ADF render before it starts a new column. If you don't enter a value, all your input elements will be shown in one column. If for example, you set the value 10, ADF will render the first 10 elements in the first column and then start a second column for items 11 through 20.

- *MaxColumns* defines how many columns are allowed—the default value is 3 for desktop applications and 2 when running on a tablet or smartphone.

If you have more elements than *Rows* times *MaxColumns*, the *MaxColumns* limitation has priority. That is, if you have 30 elements, *Rows* is 8 and *MaxColumns* is 3, ADF will adhere to the *MaxColumns* limitation and override the *Rows* setting, rendering your elements as 10 rows by 3 columns.

Using Panel Collection Layout

Another specialized layout component is the *Panel Collection Layout* (`<af:panelCollectionLayout>`). This component is intended to be used together with an `<af:table>` component for displaying multiple data records at the same time.

It contains three facets:

- The menus facet is used if you want to add extra items to the built-in menu items provided by the panel collection layout.

- The toolbar facet is used if you need a toolbar with buttons.

- The statusbar facet is used if you want to display additional information in a status bar below the table.

To use a panel collection, drop it onto your page from the *Components* window. Then, drop a collection from the Data Controls pane onto the panel collection as an ADF Table. If you have already dropped a collection as a table, you can right-click the table component and choose *Source* ➤ *Surround* and then select a *Panel Collection* from the *Surround With* dialog.

By default, the panel collection will show up as an extra line above the table. It contains a *View* menu with functionality to select which columns to display, how to sort them, and more. Figure 3-4 shows the default menu.

Figure 3-4. *Panel collection with ADF table*

You can add additional menus next to the built-in *View* menu by dropping a *Menu* component (`<af:menu>`) onto the menus facet, either in the source view or in the *Structure* panel at the bottom left of the JDeveloper window. Inside this menu, you add menu items, normally `<af:commandMenuItem>`, that invoke methods in Java Bean classes you write. We'll return to Java Beans in Chapter 5.

If you want to add buttons directly to the panel collection top bar, you drop a *Toolbar* (`<af:toolbar>`) onto the toolbar facet and then drop *Button* components (`<af:button>`) onto the toolbar.

To create a status bar below the table, you drop a *Toolbar* onto the `statusbar` facet and then place the desired component in the status bar. Often, this will be an *Output Text* with the value property set to some calculated status. In Chapter 4, we'll return to how to compute values in Java code and display the result in an *Output Text*.

Using Tabs and Accordions

If you have more information than you can fit on one page, and the user needs to be able to switch quickly back and forth among all the elements, you can consider grouping it using tabs or accordions. Both are interactive container items that contain other layout components, which again contain the actual data elements or action items the user will be interacting with.

Panel Tabbed

We already discussed the *Panel Tabbed* component at the end of Chapter 1. This component will render each detail item within it as a separate tab when running the application. When you drop a *Panel Tabbed* (`<af:panelTabbed>`) onto a page or page fragment, JDeveloper shows the *Create Panel Tabbed* wizard. In this wizard, you can define all your tabs and select where to place them (above, below, both, left, right, start, or end). The start and end locations respect your regional settings and will show to the left for left-to-right languages like English and show to the right for right-to-left languages like Arabic.

The wizard is of course just a shortcut to create multiple components at the same time. If you later decide you want another tab placement, you can change the *Position* attribute. If you find that you need an additional tab, you can add a *Show Detail Item* from the *Components* window or write or copy an `<af:showDetailItem>` tag in source view.

If all your tabs do not fit on the screen, ADF will automatically display both scroll arrows, allowing you to scroll right and left, and a *List all tabs* icon (a downward-pointing triangle).

Panel Accordion

Another layout component that allows the user to choose between different views of your application is the *Panel Accordion*. This is named after the musical instrument that can also be expanded and contracted.

When you drop a *Panel Accordion* onto a page from the *Components* window, the *Create Panel Accordion* appears. Similar to the wizard for creating a tabbed layout, this window allows you to define the *panes* you want inside the accordion. At the top of the dialog, you choose between *One pane at a time* and *Multiple panes at the same time*. If you choose to display one at a time, the open accordion will automatically close when the user selects a new one. You can of course only select *Disclosed* for one pane if you chose to have only one open. If you choose to allow the user to have multiple panes open, the *Disclosed* column changes to a check box where you can select multiple panes.

If you later want to add a new pane, simply drop a *Show Detail Item* inside the panel accordion. To change between displaying one and many panes, you change the value of the *Disclose Many* property. For each detail within the accordion, you can control whether it is initially displayed by setting the *Disclosed* property.

■ **Tip**   You can convert your layout between *Panel Tabbed* and *Panel Accordion* by changing the just the panel component. The *Show Detail Item* components work the same way in both types of panel.

Other Layout Components

Panel Grid, Panel Form, and Panel Collection are the most commonly used layout components, and Panel Tabbed and Panel Accordion can help you if you have very complex pages. In addition to these, ADF offers a long list of other layout components, including

- *Panel Stretch Layout* with a center facet for content and optional top, bottom, start, and end facets for additional information.

- *Panel Splitter* with two facets, one of which can be collapsed. This allows the user the choice between using the entire screen area on one facet or to split the screen between the two facets.

- *Show Detail* offers a collapsible area you can use for supplementary information or optional input. Note that *Show Detail* is different from *Show Detail Item. Show Detail* is used on its own, but *Show Detail Item* is used in the context of a *Panel Tabbed, Panel Accordion*, or other layout containers.

- *Decks* offer a transition between different views (like a slideshow), and *Panel Dashboard* allows you to create a layout with boxes that can be rearranged by the user.

Sometimes, you just want to adjust a little extra spacing to your layout, for example, to align items better. You can use *Spacer* components for this. These invisible components have a fixed width and height you can set in pixels.

■ **Note**   The recommended approach for alignment is to use a correctly configured *Panel Grid Layout.* Your design should not depend on *Spacers*.

Responsive Design

Responsive Design means applications that are built to change in response to available screen size. The idea is to build one application that looks good on both large desktop workstations and small tablets or even smartphones. ADF 12c release 2 (12.2.x) has two features that make this easier: *Masonry Layout* and *Match Media Behavior*.

Masonry Layout

The Masonry Layout manager dynamically arranges specially formatted detail items in a grid. While the name "masonry" might imply a fixed wall, it is actually a very dynamic layout, arranging the "bricks" when the page is first rendered, and rearranging them every time the application browser window changes in size. The ADF documentation calls the bricks *tiles*.

This kind of layout makes sense in a dashboard-type application where you have many small information elements to present. Small data visualization components like donut charts work well in a masonry layout, either by themselves or as links to other pages with more detailed information.

There are several different layout components you can use as bricks—the most common are Panel Box and Panel Group Layout. The documentation doesn't state which ones work, but most components do *not* work as bricks in a masonry layout.

■ **Tip**   When you create a masonry layout in the current version of JDeveloper (12.2.1.2.0), it is filled with two default *Panel Box* components. A default *Panel Box* can be collapsed, but the masonry layout, unfortunately, doesn't notice this, leading to a misaligned layout. Change the *Show Disclosure* property to *false* so the user can't mess up the masonry layout.

Just like Lego bricks, the bricks in a masonry layout must all have a standard size. The masonry layout has a default smallest brick of 170 × 170 pixels, and all other bricks are multiples of this size, taking into account the spacing between bricks.

Brick Size

The size of a component inside a masonry layout must be defined using the *Style Class* property. Oracle supplies eight standard sizes for us:

- AFMasonryTileSize1x1

- AFMasonryTileSize1x2

- AFMasonryTileSize1x3

- AFMasonryTileSize2x1

- AFMasonryTileSize2x2

- AFMasonryTileSize2x3

- AFMasonryTileSize3x1

- AFMasonryTileSize3x2

If none of these fit your need, the masonry layout recognizes style class names above these, all the way up to AFMasonryTileSize10x10. However, if you want to use these larger sizes, you must define the corresponding CSS classes in your skin CSS file.

The default size of a 1 × 1 brick is 170 by 170 pixels. The default border is 8 pixels, so the distance between two adjacent bricks is 16 pixels. In order for the masonry to line up correctly, larger bricks must have a size that is a multiple of the base size plus the distance between bricks. For example, the total width of two 1 × 1 bricks next to each other is 2 × 170 pixel + 2 × 8 pixel border between them. Therefore, the 2 × 1 brick is 356 pixels wide.

■ **Note**   It is possible to override the AFMasonryTileSize classes in your own CSS file, creating a masonry layout with different brick sizes. Because masonry layout is a brand-new feature in ADF 12.2 and still has some rough edges, it is not recommended to use a nonstandard brick size.

Brick Alignment at Runtime

At runtime, ADF renders a masonry layout by adding bricks in the order they are listed inside the <af:masonryLayout> tag. They are added in reading order from left to right (unless you have configured your ADF application for a right-to-left language). Bricks are added one at a time until the next brick can no longer fit in the current row. The brick that didn't fit then becomes the first brick in a new row. As soon as the layout has more than one row, ADF tries to fit the next brick into any open space in each row. Only if it does not fit anywhere, is it added to the end of the bottom row.

For example, if a wide 3x1 brick has caused ADF to start a second row, it might still be able to fit any subsequent 1x1 or 2x1 bricks into the first row. Similarly, ADF tries to fill any holes left over by bricks of different height.

Masonry Best Practice

If you have many large bricks, as shown in Figure 3-5, ADF can't really fit them together into a nice-looking layout.

Figure 3-5. *Too many large bricks in a masonry layout*

To make a masonry layout work well, you need a good supply of small (1 × 1) bricks that ADF can fit into any spaces left over by the larger bricks, as shown in Figure 3-6.

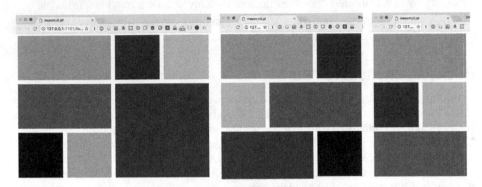

Figure 3-6. *Masonry layout with enough small bricks*

On a large monitor, a masonry layout will end up on one line, as shown in Figure 3-7, unless you limit it.

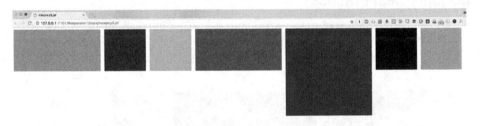

Figure 3-7. *Very wide masonry layout*

To avoid this, you can place the masonry layout inside another container with a limited with. You can place it inside a *Panel Group Layout* where you set the *InlineStyle* property to, for example, `max-width:750px`.

Screen-Dependent Formatting

The masonry layout is an automatic way of implementing responsive design—ADF fits the defined bricks into the layout as well as it can.

However, ADF also offers another way of controlling the layout of pages depending on screen size: through the `<af:matchMediaBehavior>` tag. When you place this tag inside another component, it can control some attributes of its surrounding tag. For example, you can control the *Rows* attribute of a Panel Form Layout, as shown in Listing 3-2.

Listing 3-2. Using <af:matchMediaBehavior>

```
<af:panelFormLayout id="pfl1" rows="6">
  <af:matchMediaBehavior propertyName="rows"
    matchedPropertyValue="12" mediaQuery="screen and (max-width: 768px)"/>
...
</af:panelFormLayout>
```

In this example, the *Rows* property of the *Panel Form Layout* has the default value 6, but if the screen size falls below 768 pixels, the value of *Rows* changes to 12.

The `<af:matchMediaBehavior>` attributes specify which attribute of the containing tag is to be changed (`propertyName`), and what the value is to be (`matchedPropertyValue`). The condition is placed in the `mediaQuery` property and follows standard *CSS3 media query syntax*.

It is important that the property is explicitly defined in the containing tag—in this case, that the *Panel Form Layout* has *Rows* defined. Otherwise, your application will fail with a `NullPointerException`.

In the version of ADF current when this book was written (12.2.1.2.0), the `<af:matchMediaBehavior>` tag has no documentation except a short example in the documentation—it doesn't even appear in the online tag documentation at *http://docs. oracle.com/middleware/12212/adf/tag-reference-faces/toc.htm*. It doesn't seem to be able to do much more than changing this specific attribute. It would be very useful if you could change the width of an element, but that doesn't seem to work in the current version. It would also be an excellent feature if you could change the *Rendered* property, which controls whether a specific component is shown or not.

■ **Note**   Check the documentation and the tag guide to see if the functionality of `<af:matchMediaBehavior>` has improved since this book was written.

Styling

All the ADF components have an acceptable default visual appearance. However, most organizations want to change the look in some way, and ADF supports that. Because an ADF application is a web application running in a browser, normal Cascading Style Sheet (CSS) styling works for ADF components. This section describes how to change the look of individual components.

Almost every ADF component has an *InlineStyle* property where you can write CSS styling. Some components also have a *ContentStyle* property and a few have an additional *LabelStyle* property.

There is also a *StyleClass* property where you can enter a reference to a CSS style class. Using this property requires that your application has a separate CSS file.

Inline Styles

The *InlineStyle* field is connected to the many specific CSS style fields on the six tabs below the field. You can either write CSS styling directly in the field or make selections and enter text on the tabs. JDeveloper automatically keeps the *InlineStyle* field synchronized with the many fields on the tabs, as shown in Figure 3-8.

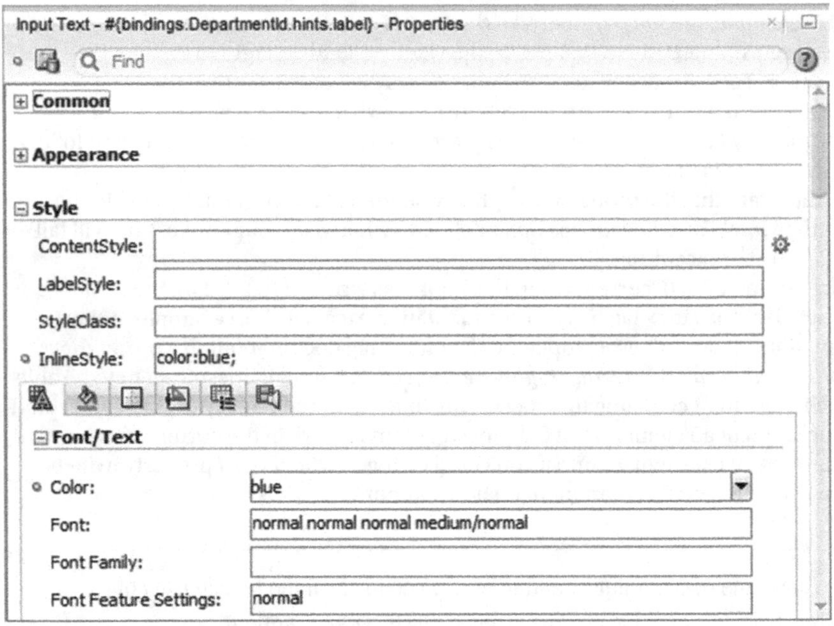

Figure 3-8. Setting InlineStyle

Unfortunately, setting the *InlineStyle* doesn't always give you the result you expect. The reason is that some ADF components become quite complicated HTML constructs when they are rendered in a browser. For example, Figure 3-9 shows what an *Input Text* component looks like at runtime in the browser when viewed with the *Developer Tools* in Google Chrome.

Figure 3-9. The HTML for an Input Text

The one component becomes an HTML table row (`<tr>`) containing one cell (`<td>`) for the label and one for the actual field. Setting an *InlineStyle* for an Input Text affects the HTML table row, but not the label cell or the input field.

Content Style

To address the problem of applying a style to the content of an item and not the whole HTML tag around it, ADF offers you the option of setting a *ContentStyle*. The CSS formatting you put in this field affects the content of the component. For example, in an Input Text component, it affects the field where the value is displayed and can be changed.

You must write proper CSS in the *ContentStyle* field—there is no typing help like you get from the six tabs with icons below the *InlineStyle* field. If you're not strong on CSS commands, you can make your selections on the tabs and then move the finished CSS expression from *InlineStyle* to *ContentStyle*. Figure 3-10 shows an example of using *ContentStyle*.

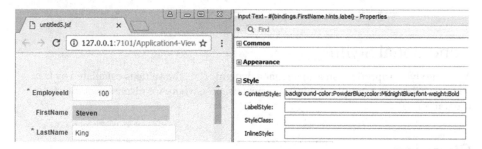

Figure 3-10. *Setting ContentStyle*

Label Style

Some of the ADF input components have a label element that is part of the component. Figure 3-9 shows that the entire input text element is a table row with two cells for label and content. Where *InlineStyle* applies to everything, and *ContentStyle* applies to the content, *LabelStyle* applies to the label text and background.

Similar to *ContentStyle*, you have to write valid CSS in the *LabelStyle* property and don't get any help from the styling tabs below the property.

Style Class

If you are adding the same styling to a lot of elements, it makes sense to store your CSS in one place and reuse it. A skin contains a CSS file, but depending on the tool you use to create your skin, you might or might not be able to add your own style classes to the skin CSS file.

Skin editor	Own CSS classes possible in skin?
Built-in JDeveloper skin editor	Yes, in source view
Theme Editor web application (from 12.2.1)	No

As described in the following section on Skinning, the *Theme Editor* is the easiest tool for changing your application skin. However, because it isolates the developer from the CSS details, it does not offer the ability to define your own style classes.

Instead, you must create a CSS file in your Common UI project and add it to your page and page fragment templates using an <af:resource> tag. The classes defined in your CSS files can then be used in the *StyleClass* property.

■ **Note**   The style class definition in the CSS file uses dot notation like .veryImportant. The *StyleClass* property is set without the dot (veryImportant).

Conditional Styling

All of the style properties can also be made dynamic (i.e., the value is calculated by Java code). We'll see an example of this in the next chapter, where we discuss user interface programming.

Skinning

The look of all ADF applications is controlled by their *skin*. Over the lifetime of ADF, ADF applications have had many different appearances. The next-to-last was the *Skyros* skin, and the latest is the *Alta* skin. Oracle recommends you use the Alta skin and follow the Alta guidelines for all new application development. This is also what Oracle is doing themselves across all products, including Application Express (APEX) and Oracle JET. So, if the organization uses other Oracle development tools than ADF, the applications will have something in common.

Oracle Alta covers many aspects of the user experience, and Oracle has created a whole web site on using Alta. It explains the visual style and provides user experience design patterns. These design patterns are based on Oracle's user experience research and explain the best way to design pages and implement specific features. You find all material on Oracle Alta at www.oracle.com/webfolder/ux/middleware/alta/index.html.

Working with Skins

Creating CSS files is a specialty in web development, and ADF skins are extracomplicated CSS files. Oracle has been trying many different things to make is reasonably easy for regular developers to create ADF skins, and it doesn't seem like they have found the final solution yet.

At the time of writing, JDeveloper is in version 12.2.1.2.0, and you can create and edit skins in two ways:

- Inside JDeveloper

- With the stand-alone Theme Editor web application

The stand-alone Theme Editor is easiest to use but does not allow you to edit every aspect of the application. The Theme Editor user interface talks of *Themes*, but a theme is the same as a skin.

In JDeveloper, you can make any change, but the JDeveloper skin editor is not as user-friendly as the theme editor. Unfortunately, you will have to choose between the two tools. Oracle documentation claims that it is possible to create a skin in JDeveloper based on a theme created in the Theme Editor, but this does not seem to work in the version of JDeveloper current at the time of writing (12.2.1.2.0).

■ **Note**   The recommended approach is to create your skin in the Theme Editor. If the capabilities of the Theme Editor prove insufficient, create a skin in the JDeveloper skin editor and copy and paste the CSS from your theme into the JDeveloper skin editor on the source tab.

Setting Up the Theme Editor

The Theme Editor is a web application (EAR file) that you get together with JDeveloper. To set it up, you need to create an application workspace in JDeveloper and configure the application to store the skins you work on:

1. Choose *File* ➤ *New* ➤ *Application* ➤ *Application from EAR file*

2. Choose the *Theme Editor* EAR file \<*jdeveloper_install_dir*>\ *jdeveloper**skineditor**skin-editor-webapp.ear* and finish the wizard

3. In JDeveloper, open the *web.xml* file and add the following context initialization parameters (the SKIN_REPOSITORY parameter might already exist):

```
<context-param>
 <description>Set this context parameter to file so that themes get
 saved to a temporary directory. Specify a directory location for
 oracle.adf.view.rich.SKIN_REPOSITORY_FILE_PATH to persist changes
 between server restarts.</description>
 <param-name>oracle.adf.view.rich.SKIN_REPOSITORY</param-name>
 <param-value>file</param-value>
</context-param>
```

```
<context-param>
 <description>Set this context parameter to a directory location where
 themes are saved. Use to persist changes between server restarts
 </description>
  <param-name>oracle.adf.view.rich.SKIN_REPOSITORY_FILE_PATH
  </param-name>
  <param-value>C:\\JDeveloper\\adfskins</param-value>
</context-param>
```

Then save and close the *web.xml* file.

The value of the SKIN_REPOSITORY_FILE_PATH is where the Theme Editor will store your skin files. On Windows, you need to write backslashes twice, as shown in the preceding. On Mac and Linux, the file path only contains forward slashes that only need to be written once, like this: /Users/sten/jdeveloper/adfskins.

Creating a Skin

If you are using a modular architecture as described in Chapter 2, you need just one application-specific skin.

If you are using an enterprise architecture, you should first create an enterprise skin named after your organization. Then, you create an application-specific skin for each application. This skin should be named after the application and extend your enterprise-level skin. Both the Theme Editor and the JDeveloper skin editor allow you to base a skin on a previously defined one.

When you have performed the setup described in the previous section, you can right-click the *index.html* file under *Web Content* in the *skin-editor* project and choose *Run*. This will start the *Theme Editor* web application in the built-in WebLogic service in JDeveloper and open a browser for you to start working on your skin. The initial page of the *Theme Editor* will look as shown in Figure 3-11.

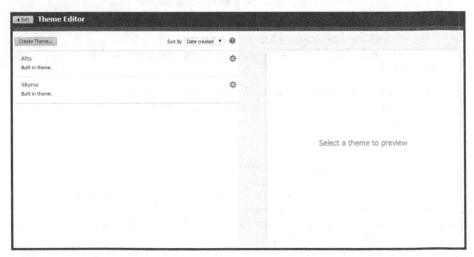

Figure 3-11. *Theme editor initial view*

From this view, you can create a new skin by clicking the *Create Theme* button.

■ **Note**   Remember that this tool uses the word "theme" to refer to an ADF skin.

You should normally base your new skins on the existing Alta skin. In an enterprise ADF architecture, your application-specific skin should be based on your enterprise skin, which should be based on the Alta skin.

Modifying a Skin

You can click your skin to bring up the skin editing page, as shown in Figure 3-12.

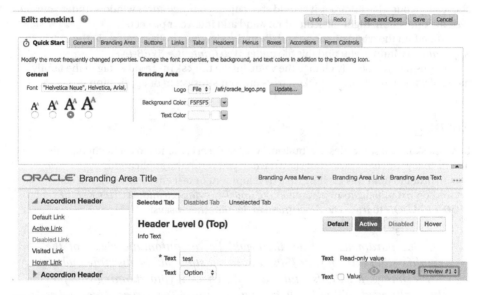

Figure 3-12.   *Theme editing window*

Using the different tabs on in this web application, you can make changes to the look of your application. The effect of your changes is shown in the lower part of the browser window, and you can toggle between multiple previews.

As mentioned previously, when you save your skin, its files will be stored in the SKIN_REPOSITORY_FILE_PATH location. There will be a directory with your skin name and version, and inside that, you find the actual CSS file for your skin. If you add (upload) any of your own resources like logos or icons, these will become part of the skin and stored in the *resources* subdirectory.

Exporting a Skin

When you are done making the necessary changes to your skin, you can export it as an ADF library with the gearwheel icon on the *Theme Editor* overview page. Your skin gets a system-generated name that you should change into something meaningful.

As with other ADF libraries, once your skin has been tested, it should be moved to your common ADF library directory for your ADF subsystems and master applications to make use of.

Using a Skin

To use a skin in a subsystem or master application, you first need to add the skin ADF library file to your application. This is done in the same way as other ADF libraries are added, as described in Chapter 2. Once you have placed it in the location you have chosen for your ADF libraries, it should show up in your *Resources* window under your file system connection. Right-click the library and add it to your project.

Then find the trinidad-config.xml file in the view/controller project. In the tree in the *Applications* window, you find this file under *Web Content* ➤ *WEB-INF*.

In this file, you simply change the value inside the `<skin-family>` tag to the family name of your skin. That's all it takes to reskin your subsystem or application.

Testing

Because skins are static files, the built-in WebLogic server tends to cache them. This means that your changes are not shown when you rerun the application.

In order to limit this caching (in a development or test environment), you can set the context initialization parameter *org.apache.myfaces.trinidad.CHECK_FILE_MODIFICATION* to *true*. The description of the parameter says:

> *"If this parameter is true, there will be an automatic check of the modification date of your JSPs, and saved state will be discarded when JSP's change. It will also automatically check if your skinning CSS files have changed without you having to restart the server. This makes development easier but adds overhead. For this reason, this parameter should be set to false when your application is deployed."*

Even though you set this parameter, you will still have to stop your application (from the Processes window) before running it again.

■ **Note** Simply right-clicking and choosing *Run* will lead to a redeployment where your skin changes do not take effect.

If you inspect a running ADF application with a tool like Firebug or Google Chrome Developer Tools, you will see that all styles have short names like xrs. This is an optimization that ADF automatically makes for performance reasons, but during development, you can disable it to see the full style class names. To do so, change the *org. apache.myfaces.trinidad.DISABLE_CONTENT_COMPRESSION* parameter to *true*.

Working with the JDeveloper Skin Editor

If you need more skinning power than the Theme Editor offers, you can create an ADF skin within JDeveloper. When you open the skin CSS files, JDeveloper recognizes that the file is part of a skin and shows it in a specialized view.

For skins based on Oracle's older Skyros skin, JDeveloper shows a skin view that contains a *Design* tab, as shown in Figure 3-13.

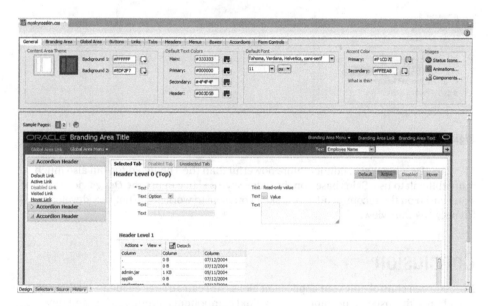

Figure 3-13. *The skin Design view in JDeveloper*

On this tab, JDeveloper attempts to show the effect of the changes you make. The skin view also has a Selectors view (described in the following) and a Source view that shows the raw CSS file.

Skins based on Oracle's newer Alta skin are not displayed with a *Design* tab. Instead, you work on the *Selectors* tab shown in Figure 3-14. On this tab, you can select elements of ADF design in the tree to the left, make changes in the *Properties* window (not shown in Figure 3-13), and then see the result to the right.

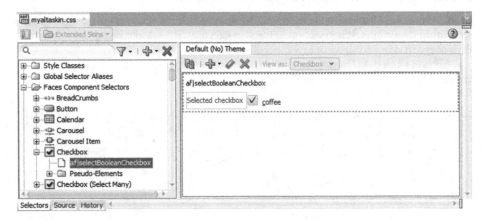

Figure 3-14. *The skin Selectors view in JDeveloper*

The JDeveloper skin editor is more powerful than the Theme Editor, but also much more difficult to use. Skins based on the older Skyros skin can use the *Design* view, but for skins based on the recommended Alta skin, you have to work in the not very developer friendly *Selectors* view.

Conclusion

Now you can control how your application looks. You can arrange elements on the screen and change the visual appearance of individual components through styling and the entire application through the use of ADF skins. In the next chapter, we'll see how to add presentation logic to your application.

CHAPTER 4

Business Logic

Much of the core functionality of your application will be implemented in the business components. ADF offers a range of ways to add simple business logic without writing code, but most of what makes your application unique will be implemented in Java and/or Groovy.

■ **Note**   Groovy is a scripting language that integrates with Java and is run in a Java Virtual Machine just like Java code. Groovy has a simpler syntax than Java, making it a good choice for code snippets used to define default values or programmatic validation, for example.

One of the hard things about writing enterprise Java applications is creating an object hierarchy that fits the specific business problem you are trying to solve. However, this is not necessary in an Oracle ADF application. With the concept of entity objects, view objects, and application modules, Oracle ADF establishes a best practice object hierarchy, and you just need to fill in the blanks by overriding or adding methods to ADF Java objects. This is one of the secrets that make ADF so productive even for developers with little Java knowledge.

Logic in Entity Objects

Closest to the database we find the entity objects. The logic you add to entity objects will apply throughout the entire application because all data access goes through these objects. ADF automatically creates instances of business component classes whenever they are needed. As described in Chapter 2, you should make use of the option to create your own business component base classes extending the Oracle-supplied classes.

© Sten Vesterli 2017
S. Vesterli, *Oracle ADF Survival Guide*, DOI 10.1007/978-1-4842-2820-3_4

The amount of Java code you need to write in these custom base classes will depend on your application needs:

- If the declarative functionality of the ADF entity object is sufficient, you don't need to add logic to the base classes or create specific Java classes for entity objects. In this case, ADF simply creates and configures an instance of the relevant business component base class.

- If you want to change how *all* entity objects work, you override methods in your entity object base class (in the BCBase project in your foundation workspace).

- If you want to change how a *specific* entity object works, you need to create a Java class for that entity object, extending the base class.

Some logic (e.g., calculating default values or programming validations) does not require Java code at all, but can be handled with simpler Groovy scripts.

Default Values

To set a dummydefault value for an attribute, you select it on the *Attributes* tab in the entity object and then fill in the *Default Value* section at the bottom right of the *Details* tab. Figure 4-1 shows how to define a default value using a Groovy expression.

Figure 4-1. *Defining an attribute default value using a Groovy expression*

In a Groovy expression, you can refer to attributes in the current entity object using just the attribute name, use the special `adf` object, and perform normal calculations and logic. In the preceding example, we use the built-in `adf.currentDate` function to provide a default value for `HireDate`. Refer to the section "Using Groovy Scripting Language with Business Components" in the Oracle manual *Developing Fusion Web Applications with Oracle Application Development Framework* for more on the built-in `adf` object and how to use Groovy expressions.

■ **Tip**   The *Help* button in the *Expression Editor* shows you some basic help information and contains a link to the preceding section in the manual.

Groovy expressions are stored in separate .bcs (Business Components Script) files. In some places in ADF business components, a Groovy script shows up as a hyperlink you can click to open the .bcs file in a full editor window.

Validation

Much of the business logic in typical applications handles data validation. ADF offers several ways to make it easy to define validations of attributes or entire entity objects.

Declarative Validation

To add validation to an entity object, open it and choose the *Business Rules* tab to the left. You can then right-click either the *Entity Validator* node to specify validation for the entire entity object or an individual attribute to add a validator for that attribute. The *Add Validation Rule* dialog appears as shown in Figure 4-2.

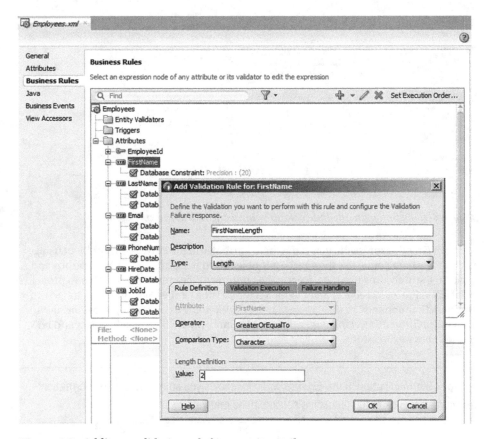

Figure 4-2. *Adding a validation rule for an entity attribute*

There are many types of validation rules available:

- Collection (only entity level)

- Compare

- Key Exists

- Length

- List

- Method

- Range

- Regular Expression

- Script Expression

- UniqueKey (only entity level)

The *Compare* validation is very useful and can compare an attribute value to a literal, another attribute in the same entity object, an attribute in another entity object, or even the result of an SQL query.

Length and *Range* validations provide simple checks on an attribute value against literal values.

Key Exists and *List* validations validate that an attribute exists as a key in some other entity, or that the attribute is part of a specific list of allowed values. You should not depend on these validations, but instead create a user interface that only allows the user to select valid values. Similarly, you should autogenerate unique keys and not depend on the entity-level *UniqueKey* validation.

For validating advanced formats, you can use *Regular Expression* validations. These expressions are written in a very specific syntax and allow you to specify rules like "two uppercase letters, followed by one to four digits." JDeveloper offers you a few examples, including e-mail validation, which looks like this: `[a-zA-Z0-9._%+-]+@[a-zA-Z0-9.-]+\.[a-zA-Z]{2,4}`. As this example makes obvious, it takes a little work to get used to this syntax. While an Internet search is likely to provide you with a regular expression for most validations, someone on your team should make the effort to understand regular expression syntax.

At the entity level, you can also create a *Collection* validation. This is a rather specialized validation that validates a collection of child records. For example, a *Collection* validation on a *Department* entity object might restrict the sum of the salary of all employees in the department. To be able to implement *Collection* validation, the relationship between the parent and the children must be configured in a specific way:

1. An association must exist between the entity object you validate and the entity object containing the collection of children.

2. The association must be of *Composition* type. This type is not the default, but is set on the *Relationship* tab in the association, where the *Composition Association* check box must be checked.

When creating a *Collection* validation, you are asked to select an operation, an *Accessor*, an attribute, an operator, and a comparison value, as shown in Figure 4-3.

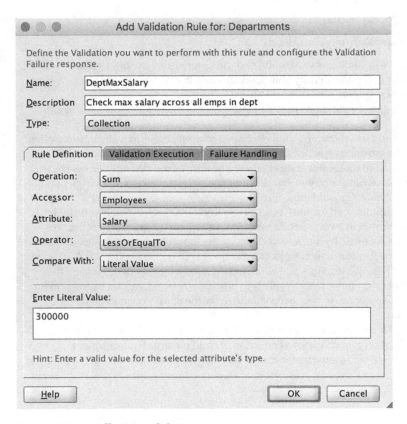

Figure 4-3. *A Collection validation*

If both preconditions are met, an accessor for the child entity object should show up on the Accessor list. Once you have selected the accessor, you can select the attribute in the child entity object to be validated against.

Script Expression Validation

You can also select validations of type *Script Expression* and write a *Groovy* expression. This programming language has a Java-like syntax and can be used in many places in ADF. The Oracle manual *Developing Fusion Web Applications with Oracle Application Development Framework* describes how to use Groovy for validation, default values, and much more. The expression must return either true (for validation success) or false (for validation failure). Alternatively, you can call adf.error.raise() or adf.error.warn() in case you might need to issue either an error or a warning.

Method Validation

If none of the declarative validations or script validation fit your needs, you can always create a *Method* validation. To do this, select type *Method* and leave the *Create and Select Method* check box checked, as shown in Figure 4-4.

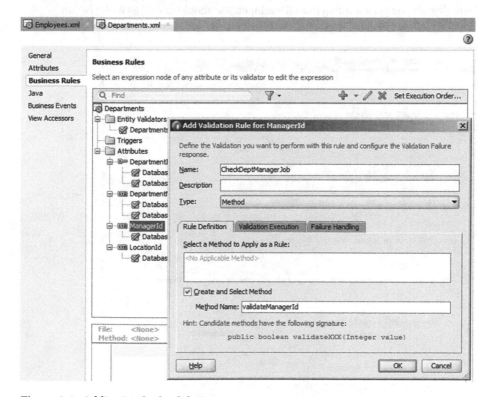

Figure 4-4. *Adding Method validation*

If you have not already created a Java class for your entity object, JDeveloper will ask if you want the class created. In the class, a validation method will be created with the right name and signature:

- An attribute validation must have the form `public boolean validateXXX(YYY value)`, where XXX is the name of the attribute and YYY is a datatype matching the attribute.

- An entity validation must have the form `public boolean validateZZZ()`, where ZZZ is the name of the entity object.

Naturally, you need to return `true` for validation success and `false` if the validation failed.

Failure Handling

If you try to close the *Add Validation* dialog without defining a message on the *Failure Handling* tab, you get a warning from JDeveloper. You should always go to the *Failure Handling* tab shown in Figure 4-5 to define the message associated with a validation failure.

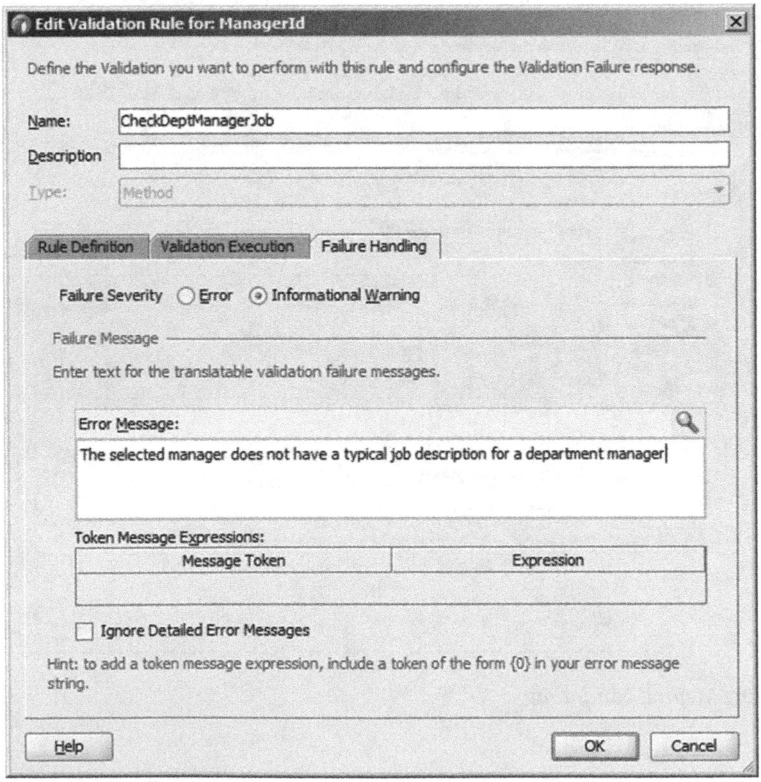

Figure 4-5. Defining a message for validation failure

On this tab, you decide whether a validation failure should be considered an error or a warning. Errors prevent the application from continuing and are shown with a red border around the offending attribute. Warnings are shown with an orange border, and the user can decide to ignore the warning and continue committing the value to the database (for example).

You provide a message and can even define variable *tokens* by using curly brackets { } in the text. For every set of curly brackets you use, a corresponding line appears in the *Token Message Expressions* table, allowing you to enter an expression that will be evaluated and inserted into the message at runtime.

Using Triggers

A new feature in ADF 12c is the ability to define entity-level *triggers*. These are similar to entity-level validations and are also added on the *Business Rules* tab. A trigger is a Groovy validation expression that is executed when the triggering condition occurs. The list of triggering conditions includes

- Before and after insert

- Before and after update

- Before and after delete

- Before and after rollback

- Before commit

- After the transaction is posted to the database

The Groovy expression you write is by default *untrusted*. Normal Groovy will run just fine, and you can call Java general-purpose APIs. However, you can't use java.io.file (for example) to read from a file. You also can't call methods defined on your entity objects from Groovy expressions.

If you want to explicitly mark your Groovy script as trustworthy, you have to find the reference to the script in the XML view of your entity object (on the *Source* tab). There will be a line trustMode="untrusted" that you can change to trustMode="trusted".

If you want to call a method you have written yourself, you can also annotate that method with @AllowUntrustedScriptAccess to indicate that it is OK that untrusted scripts call the method. Refer to the section "What You May Need to Know About Untrusted Groovy Expressions" in the Oracle manual *Developing Fusion Web Applications with Oracle Application Development Framework* for an example of how to configure trust in a Java class.

Creating a Java Object

In order to add business logic to a specific entity object, you need a Java class for the object. If you haven't created one already by defining a method type validation, you can create one by going to the *Java* tab of your entity object and clicking the edit (pencil) icon to bring up the *Select Java Options* dialog, as shown in Figure 4-6.

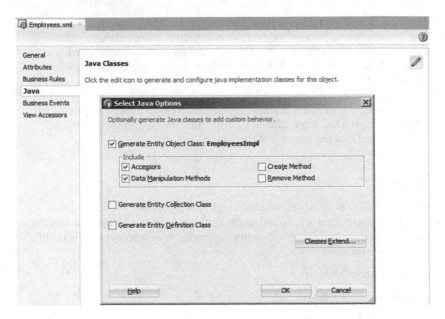

Figure 4-6. *Creating Java for an entity object*

You will normally only create the *Entity Object Class*. It is very rare that an application needs to create its own *Entity Collection Class* (which handles the caching of data) or its own *Entity Definition Class* (which defines the inner working of the entity object).

Your choices in the *Include* section for *Entity Object Class* decide which methods JDeveloper will place into the entity object Java class. The Java class will extend the relevant business component base class, and all the methods added will call the relevant methods from the base class. This means that the entity object will work exactly as it did before you generated Java—but now you have a Java class for one specific entity object where you can add your own logic.

The *Include* section gives you the following options:

- **Accessors:** This creates setter and getter methods for all attributes in the entity object. All of these methods call setAttributeInternal() and getAttributeInternal() to maintain default functionality.

- **Data Manipulation Methods:** This creates a doDML() method and a lock() method. The doDML() method is invoked as part of standard ADF processing whenever the ADF framework wishes to send an INSERT, UPDATE, or DELETE statement to the database. Later in this chapter, we will see an example of how this method can be used. The lock() method is invoked when ADF wishes to establish a database lock on a specific record.

- **Create Method:** This creates a local create() method that takes an AttributeList object as parameter. It is called when ADF wants to create a new record, before the doDML() that happens right before the actual INSERT statement is sent to the database. Customizations often involve modifying the AttributeList to add missing values or manipulate the values passed from the user interface.

- **Remove Method:** This creates a local remove() method that is called whenever ADF wants to remove a record, before the doDML() call that happens before a DELETE is sent to the database.

You can always add individual methods inside the generated class by right-clicking in the source code and choosing Source ➤ Override Methods. This will bring up the Override Methods dialog shown in Figure 4-7.

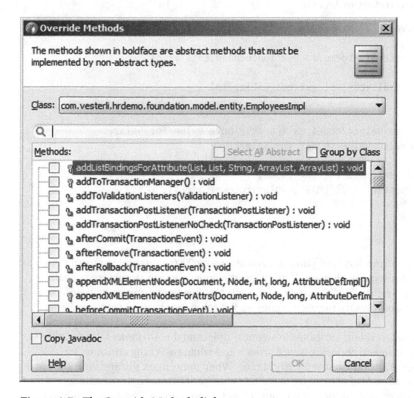

Figure 4-7. The Override Methods dialog

From this dialog, you can select one or more methods to override. This makes JDeveloper add those methods to your entity object Java class so you can modify standard behavior.

■ **Caution**   If you use the edit (pencil) icon to bring up the Select Java Options dialog again and *deselect* a check box, JDeveloper will delete the corresponding methods without warning, including any code you have added. Should this happen to you, use the *History* tab at the bottom of the Java class to find the previous version.

Accessors

If you generate accessors for an attribute, you can modify the value being stored in the setXXX() method and modify the return value in the getXXX() method.

For example, you could modify the setEmail() method to always convert the value to lowercase, as shown in Listing 4-1.

Listing 4-1. Overriding an Accessor

```
package com.vesterli.hrdemo.foundation.model.entity;
...
import com.vesterli.hrdemo.foundation.bcbase.EntityImpl;
...
public class EmployeesImpl extends EntityImpl {
...
  /**
   * Sets <code>value</code> as the attribute value for Salary.
   * @param value value to set the Salary
   */
  public void setEmail (String value) {
    setAttributeInternal(EMAIL, value.toLowerCase());
  }
...
}
```

If you want to mask values, you can override the getXXX() method to return a masked value for some or all users. For String attributes, you can simply override the getter method to return ****** instead of the actual value. For numeric attributes like Salary, you can only return numeric values, so the solution is to use a *transient* String attribute.

You can add transient attributes to an entity object on the *Attributes* tab by clicking the green plus icon and choosing *New Attribute* and adding a String attribute, for example with the attribute name SalaryString. When done, mark the attribute *Transient* on the *Details* tab so ADF will not try to include it in the SQL sent to the database.

When you create *Accessors* for an entity object, a setter and getter method is also created for transient attributes. You can add logic to the getSalaryString() method to return the true value only to users with the salary-admin-role and a series of asterisks if the user does not have this role. This is shown in Listing 4-2.

Listing 4-2. Masking Values with a Transient Attribute

```
package com.vesterli.hrdemo.foundation.model.entity;
...
import com.vesterli.hrdemo.foundation.bcbase.EntityImpl;
import oracle.adf.share.ADFContext;
import oracle.adf.share.security.SecurityContext;
...
public class EmployeesImpl extends EntityImpl {
  /**
   * Gets the attribute value for Salary, using the alias name Salary.
   * @return the value of Salary
   */
  public BigDecimal getSalary() {
    throw new JboException("Internal error reading Salary");
  }

  /**
   * Sets <code>value</code> as the attribute value for Salary.
   * @param value value to set the Salary
   */
  public void setSalary(BigDecimal value) {
    throw new JboException("Internal error writing Salary");
  }

  /**
   * Gets the attribute value for SalaryString,
   * using the alias name SalaryString.
   * @return the value of SalaryString
   */
  public String getSalaryString() {
    ADFContext actx = ADFContext.getCurrent();
    SecurityContext sctx = actx.getSecurityContext();
    if (sctx.isUserInRole("salary-admin-role")) {
      return ((BigDecimal) getAttributeInternal(SALARY)).toString();
    } else {
      return "*******";
    }
  }

  /**
   * Sets <code>value</code> as the attribute value for SalaryString.
   * @param value value to set the SalaryString
   */
  public void setSalaryString(String value) {
    try {
      BigDecimal sal = new BigDecimal(value);
      ADFContext actx = ADFContext.getCurrent();
```

```
        SecurityContext sctx = actx.getSecurityContext();
        if (sctx.isUserInRole("salary-admin-role")) {
          setAttributeInternal(SALARY, sal);
        } else {
          throw new JboException("User not allowed to change salary");
        }
      } catch (NumberFormatException e) {
        throw new JboException("Salary must be numeric");
      }
    }
    ...
  }
```

The listing also overrides the setter, taking the String value and converting into the necessary BigDecimal. It then implements the same access control logic you saw in the previous listing before calling the internal method to set the actual Salary attribute that corresponds to the database column. With both a custom setter and getter implemented, the user interface can work with this SalaryString attribute instead of the original Salary.

■ **Tip**   To prevent a UI developer from accidentally using the original Salary attribute, the code in Listing 4-2 throws an exception if the application tries to manipulate that attribute directly. You can also set the *Display* property of the Salary attribute to *Hide* (on the *UI Hints* tab) to further reduce the risk of a developer using it.

Working with the Database
Handling Database Triggers

Your database might contain triggers that change values after insert or update. If this is the case, you need to tell the entity object to expect these changes and make sure it updates itself. This is done for each attribute on the *Attributes* tab. On the *Details* subtab, you check the *Refresh on Insert* and/or *Refresh on Update* check boxes, as shown in Figure 4-8.

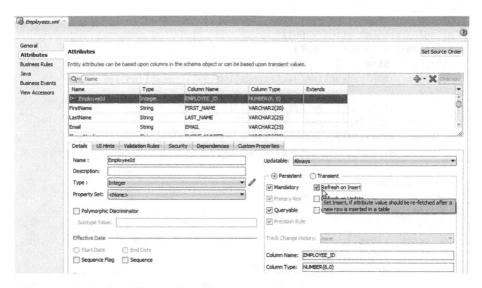

Figure 4-8. Refresh attribute on insert

This setting tells ADF to reread that attribute from the database after an insert or an update, respectively.

In an Oracle database, triggers are often used to provide primary key values. In this case, you need to set *Refresh after Insert.* When working with an Oracle database, ADF makes use of the Oracle-specific RETURNING … INTO clause to get updated values back from the database in one roundtrip. For other databases, it will take an extra roundtrip from the application server to the database to refresh the attributes.

Calling Stored Procedures

When you override the doDML() method, JDeveloper automatically places a call to super.doDML() in your entity object Java class. This ensures that normal ADF entity object processing takes place, sending an INSERT, UPDATE, or DELETE SQL statement to the database.

However, you remove this call if you don't want this to happen. This can be useful for example if you want all inserts into the table to be handled by a stored procedure in the database. In this case, you want ADF to call that procedure instead of sending an INSERT to the database. For example, if you have an EMP_API package containing a procedure INSERT_REC taking four parameters, this could look as shown in Listing 4-3.

Listing 4-3. Calling a Stored Procedure in doDML()

```
/**
 * Custom DML update/insert/delete logic here.
 * @param operation the operation type
 * @param e the transaction event
 */
```

```
protected void doDML(int operation, TransactionEvent e) {
  CallableStatement cstmt = null;
  if (operation == DML_INSERT) {
    String insStmt = "{call emp_api.insert_rec(?,?,?,?)}";
    cstmt = getDBTransaction().createCallableStatement(insStmt, 0);
    try {
      cstmt.setString(1, getFirstName());
      cstmt.setString(2, getLastName());
      cstmt.setString(3, getJobId());
      cstmt.setInteger(4, getDepartmentId());
    }
    catch (Exception ex) {
      // Handle SQL exceptions
    } finally {
      try {
        cstmt.close();
      } catch (SQLException ex) {
        // if error closing, ignore
      }
    }
  } else {
    super.doDML(operation, e);
  }
}
```

This code first checks if the statement is an INSERT. If so, it gets the current
transaction context and creates a CallableStatement with an SQL CALL statement
calling a stored procedure called INSERT_REC in the EMP_API package. As part of the
statement, question marks indicate parameters. After the statement object is created,
the attribute values from the entity object are connected to the parameters with some
setString() calls, and the statement is executed.

If the operation was not an INSERT, normal doDML() processing is handled in the
else branch with a call to super.doDML().

Replacing Standard Database Operations

Another place where overriding the doDML() method comes in handy is if you want to
implement logical deletes instead of actually deleting a record. This means that your
table and entity object needs an extra column indicated if the record has been deleted,
and every attempt to send a DELETE to the database must be intercepted and changed to
an UPDATE that sets the delete indicator attribute. If you create a new database column
DELETED_YN with a corresponding attribute in the entity object, the code could look as
shown in Listing 4-4.

Listing 4-4. Implementing Logical Delete

```
package com.vesterli.hrdemo.foundation.model.entity;
...
public class DepartmentsImpl extends EntityImpl {
  ...

  /**
   * Add entity remove logic in this method.
   */
  public void remove() {
    setDeletedYn("Y");
    super.remove();
  }
  ...

  /**
   * Custom DML update/insert/delete logic here.
   * @param operation the operation type
   * @param e the transaction event
   */
  protected void doDML(int operation, TransactionEvent e) {
    if (operation == DML_DELETE) {
      operation = DML_UPDATE;
    }
    super.doDML(operation, e);
  }

  /**
   * Gets the attribute value for DeletedYn, using the alias name DeletedYn.
   * @return the value of DeletedYn
   */
  public String getDeletedYn() {
    return (String) getAttributeInternal(DELETEDYN);
  }

  /**
   * Sets <code>value</code> as the attribute value for DeletedYn.
   * @param value value to set the DeletedYn
   */
  public void setDeletedYn(String value) {
    setAttributeInternal(DELETEDYN, value);
  }
  ...
}
```

The doDML() method simply replaces a DELETE with an UPDATE, and the remove()
method sets the attribute indicating that the record hard been deleted.

> ■ **Tip** Because records that are logically deleted remain in the database, your view object will have to filter out the records that have been logically deleted. See the section "Permanent Filtering" later in the following section on view object logic for an example.

Logic in View Objects

While the bulk of entity object logic is found in one class, view object logic is found in two classes:

- **View object classes:** These represent the query or whole data set of the view object, and the built-in functionality of these objects relates to all the records. Examples of functionality in view object classes are changing sort order, view criteria, or executing the query.

- **View row classes:** These represent individual rows in the record set defined by the view object. The functionality in these objects is related to one row. The typical function you will override in a view row object is an accessor.

Creating Java Objects

Similar to the way you create Java objects for entity objects, you create Java objects for view objects on the *Java* tab of the object by clicking the edit (pencil) icon. This brings the *Select Java Options* dialog for view objects shown in Figure 4-9.

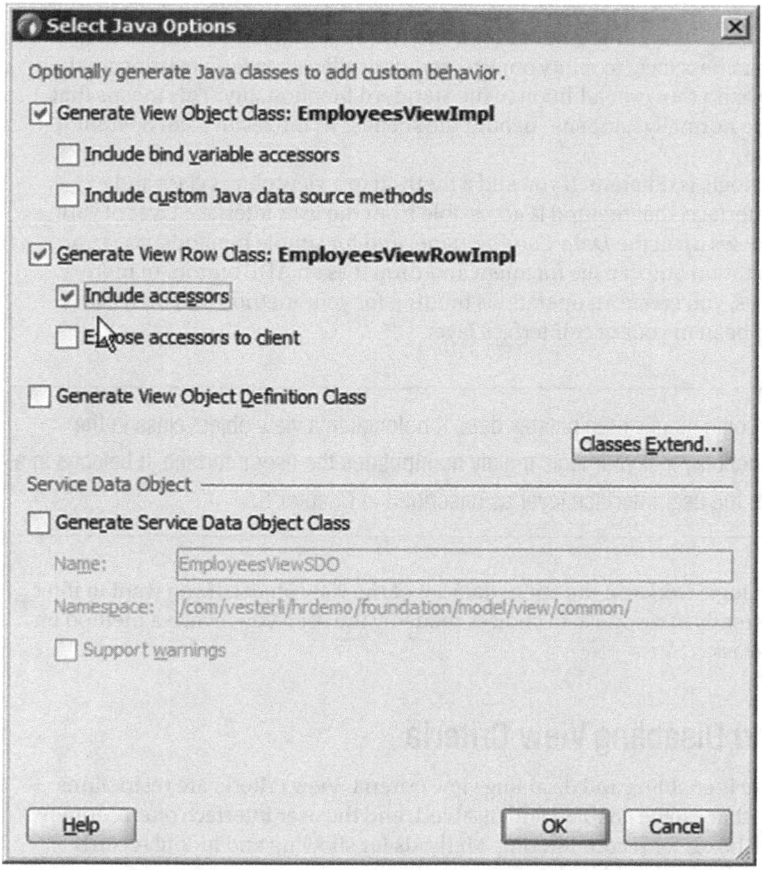

Figure 4-9. *Creating Java for a view object*

From this dialog, you can create both a *View Object Class* and a *View Row Class* and select which methods you want JDeveloper to add to the generated class. You can always edit the code later or override methods with *Source ➤ Override Methods*.

■ **Caution** If you bring up Select Java Options dialog again and *deselect* a check box, JDeveloper will unceremoniously delete the corresponding methods, including any of your code. If you lose code in this way, use the *History* tab in the Java class to revert to a previous version.

View Object Class Logic

When you add business logic to entity objects, you typically *override* an existing method to make ADF do extra things in addition to the standard functionality. This means that entity object logic normally happens "behind the scenes" as the result of an operation started elsewhere.

View object logic is different. If you add a method to a view object class and create a client interface, that method is accessible from the user interface layer of your application. It shows up in the *Data Controls* pane, and for simple methods, you can just drag the operation onto a page fragment and drop it as an ADF button. In more complicated cases, you create an operations binding for your method and then call it from a managed bean in your user interface layer.

■ **Note**   If your logic mainly manipulates data, it belongs in a view object class in the business component layer. If your logic mainly manipulates the user interface, it belongs in a managed bean in the user interface layer as described in Chapter 5.

View object logic works on the entire data set of the view object. If you want to filter or sort data differently in response to choices made by the user, you invoke a method on the view object class.

Enabling and Disabling View Criteria

A typical use case is enabling and disabling view criteria. View criteria are restrictions on a view object that can be enabled and disabled, and the user interface often contains buttons or check boxes for record filtering. Methods for showing and hiding records based on a view criterion could look as shown in Listing 4-5.

Listing 4-5. Changing View Criteria in a View Object Class

```
package com.vesterli.hrdemo.deptemp.model.view;
...
import com.vesterli.hrdemo.foundation.bcbase.ViewObjectImpl;
...
public class DepartmentsViewImpl extends ViewObjectImpl
    implements DepartmentsView {
  ...
  public void showDeleted() {
    removeViewCriteria("DontShowDeleted");
    executeQuery();
  }
```

```
public void dontShowDeleted() {
  ViewCriteria vc = getViewCriteria("DontShowDeleted");
  applyViewCriteria(vc);
  executeQuery();
}
...
}
```

Note that changing the data in the view object is not automatically reflected in the user interface. If for instance you call one of these methods from a button, you need to set the *Partial Triggers* property of the element showing the data (e.g., a *Table* component) to point to the button that changes the view criteria. The concept of partial page rendering and the partial triggers property will be explained in Chapter 5.

Permanent Filtering

In the entity object example earlier in this chapter, you saw how a logical delete could be implemented in the entity object. This method leaves logically deleted records in the database, and to prevent them from being shown to the user, you can have your view object filter out these deleted objects. This could be done for example with a view criterion, as shown in Figure 4-10.

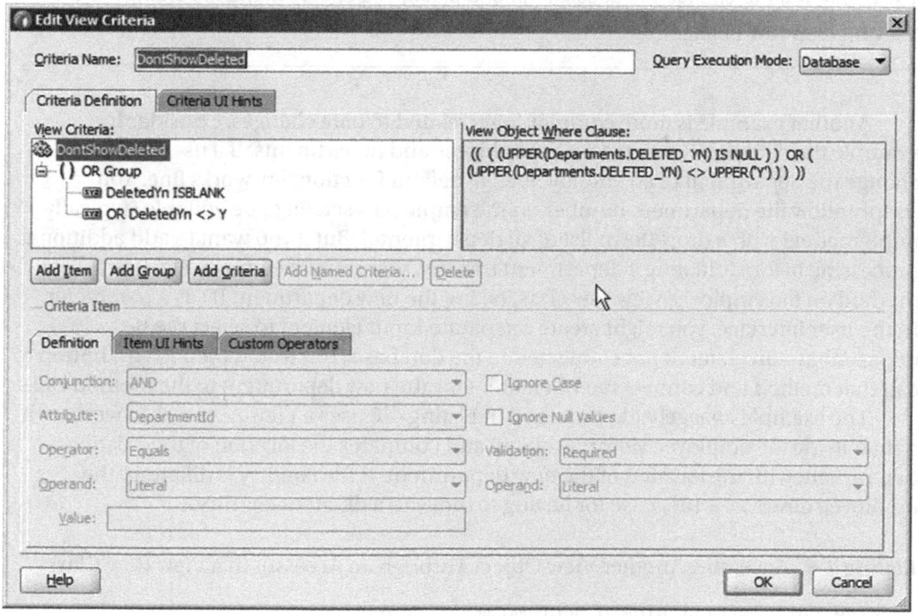

Figure 4-10. A view criterion for filtering out logically deleted records

You can add this view criterion permanently to the view object instance in the application module to prevent the deleted records from ever being shown to the user. To do this, open the *Data Model* tab of the application module and select the instance of the Departments view object. Then, click *Edit* to bring up the *Edit View Instance* dialog where you can apply the view criteria permanently in this view object instance.

View Row Class Logic

While the view object class works on the entire data set, the view row class methods work on individual records. This means that modifying data and responding to data changes belong in the view row class.

A typical change you make in the view row class is to override one or more accessor methods (setter and/or getter for specific attributes). If you check the *Include accessors* check box in the *Select Java Options* dialog, JDeveloper will automatically create accessor methods for all attributes in the view object. It doesn't cost you any performance to have a lot of accessor methods in your view row class, but it does make the code larger and it will take more time to find the method you want to change.

■ **Note**   You can also override the accessors in an entity object. If you want the change to apply throughout the entire application, you should override the accessor in the entity object. If you only want to change the accessor in one place, you should make the change in the relevant view row object.

Another example is more complex logic related to data changes. Consider for example the default HR schema with employees and departments. If a user can freely change the department of an employee, ADF default functionality works fine. You simply allow the department number on the employees screen to be editable (typically implemented with a drop-down list of all departments). But if you want to add additional processing before initiating a department transfer, you could create a changeDept() method on the employee view row class, taking the new department ID as a parameter. In the user interface, you might create a separate input element to select the new department—an element not connected to the database. You would then have a button to call that method and connect the UI element for the new department to the method call.

The example changeDept() method in Listing 4-6 uses a View Accessor to work with data outside the employee view row object and compares the location of the existing department with the location of the new department. If the country is different, the employee deserves a 10% raise for having to move to a different country.

Listing 4-6. Accessing Another View Object Through an Accessor in a View Row Class

```
package com.vesterli.hrdemo.deptemp.model.view;

import com.vesterli.hrdemo.deptemp.model.view.common.EmployeesVORow;
import com.vesterli.hrdemo.foundation.model.entity.DepartmentsImpl;
```

```java
import com.vesterli.hrdemo.foundation.bcbase.ViewRowImpl;
...
import oracle.jbo.Key;
import oracle.jbo.Row;
import oracle.jbo.RowSet;

public class EmployeesVORowImpl extends ViewRowImpl
    implements EmployeesVORow {
  ...

  public void changeDept(Integer newDeptId) {
    RowSet rs = getDepartmentsVO1();
    Row row = null;
    Object[] keyVals = new Object[1];
    keyVals[0] = getDepartmentId();
    Key oldDeptKey = new Key(keyVals);
    row = rs.getRow(oldDeptKey);
    String oldCountryId = (String)row.getAttribute("CountryId");
    keyVals[0] = newDeptId;
    Key newDeptKey = new Key(keyVals);
    row = rs.getRow(newDeptKey);
    String newCountryId = (String)row.getAttribute("CountryId");
    if (!oldCountryId.equals(newCountryId)) {
      setSalary(getSalary().multiply(new BigDecimal(1.1))
          .setScale(0, BigDecimal.ROUND_HALF_UP));
    }
  }
  ...

  /**
   * Sets <code>value</code> as attribute value for SALARY using the alias
     name Salary.
   * @param value value to set the SALARY
   */
  public void setSalary(BigDecimal value) {
    setAttributeInternal(SALARY, value);
  }
  ...

  /**
   * Gets the view accessor <code>RowSet</code> DepartmentsVO1.
   */
  public RowSet getDepartmentsVO1() {
    return (RowSet) getAttributeInternal(DEPARTMENTSVO1);
  }
  ...
}
```

The changeDept() method first uses a view accessor to get a handle to all of the rows in the DepartmentsVO1 view object instance. How to create accessors is described in the following section. The code then first creates a Key object for the old department and retrieves the country ID for that department, and then creates another Key to retrieve the country of the new department. If they are different, the salary of the current view row is set to 1.1 times the current salary, thus implementing a 10% raise when an employee is moved to a department in another country.

View Accessors

For a view row class to be able to access other view row objects, there must be an *accessor* to that object. This is created from the Accessors tab in the view object by clicking the green plus icon. In the *View Accessors* dialog shown in Figure 4-11, you can choose which accessors you want to create.

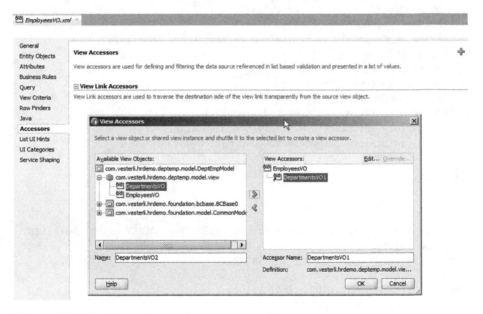

Figure 4-11. *Creating a view accessor*

There must be an association between the underlying entity objects so that JDeveloper and ADF can figure out how to get from a record in one view object to a record in another.

Logic in Application Modules

The last part of the business component layer is the application modules, and you can also create your own Java objects implementing your application modules.

You create a Java class for an application module from the Java tab, as shown in Figure 4-12.

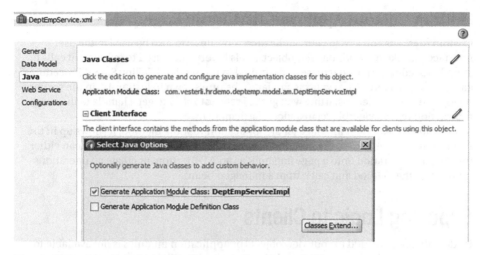

Figure 4-12. *Creating a Java class for an application module*

Application modules contain methods that you might want to override, and you might also want to add your own business logic to application modules.

Overriding Application Module Functionality

Application modules contain a collection of view object instances and control the database transaction. Therefore, many of the methods typically overridden in application-specific application module classes relate to the database transaction or connection.

When overriding application module methods, you normally want to change the behavior of the entire application (i.e., every application module). For this reason, application module methods are typically overridden in the base class that you base all your application modules on. Refer to Chapter 2 for more on specifying your own business component base classes.

The method most often overridden in application modules classes is prepareSession(), which is invoked when an application module is first created. Because application modules can be shared among multiple ADF sessions, it is also executed whenever an application module is given to a new ADF session.

This can be used if you want to perform some database initialization every time the application module connects to the database. You might want to set package variables, alter the SQL session (e.g., to start SQL tracing), or establish a session context for use with Oracle Virtual Private Database (VPD).

The application module also contains methods like beforeCommit(), beforeRollback(), afterCommit(), and afterRollback() that you can override to implement custom transaction handling.

Adding Custom Application Module Logic

Custom methods you add to your application modules can also be used in the user interface just like methods on view objects. This is very often used to implement calls to stored procedures in the database as described in the section "Calling Stored Procedures" earlier in this chapter. The syntax is similar to the one shown in Listing 4-3 in the section on logic in entity objects, starting with getDBTransaction() to get a handle to the current transaction that all view object instances participate in.

If you create a client interface for an application module method, it shows up in the *Data Controls* pane next to the built-in *Commit* and *Rollback* operations. You can either just drag the operation onto a page fragment as an ADF button, or create an operations binding for the method and call it from a managed bean.

Exposing Logic to Clients

By default, logic you add to your view objects or application modules is not available to the user interface layer. In order to make your methods available, you need to create a client interface from the *Java* tab of your view object or application module. Figure 4-13 shows creating a client interface for a view object.

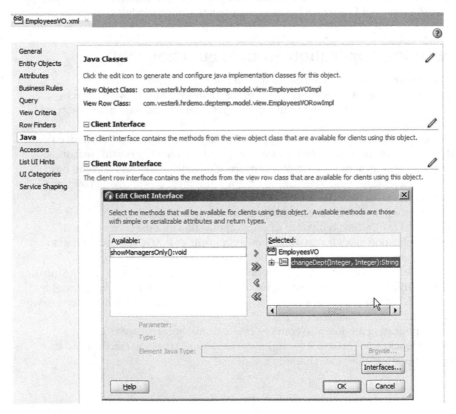

Figure 4-13. *Creating a client interface*

For a view object, you can create client interfaces for both the view object class and the view row class. For application modules, there is only one type of client interface. All the methods in the class show up on the left side of the *Edit Client Interface* dialog, and you shuffle the ones you want to be exposed to the *Selected* box to the right.

When you have exposed your methods like this, they show up in the Data Control panel next to the attributes, as shown in Figure 4-14.

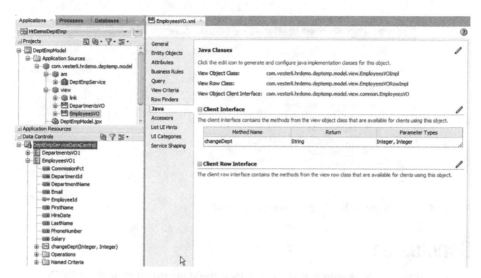

Figure 4-14. *A client method exposed in the Data Controls pane*

Once your methods show up in the Data Controls pane, they can be dragged onto pages or page fragments and dropped as ADF action elements (button or command link). If you want to use a method from a Java Bean in the user interface, you need to create an Action binding from the Binding tab on the relevant page, as shown in Figure 4-15. We'll return to using Java beans in the user interface in Chapter 5.

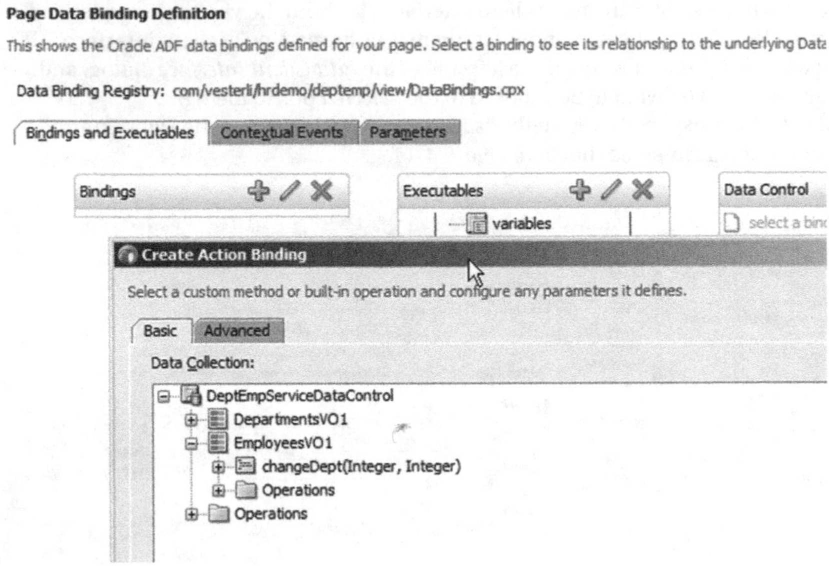

Page Data Binding Definition

This shows the Oracle ADF data bindings defined for your page. Select a binding to see its relationship to the underlying Data

Data Binding Registry: com/vesterli/hrdemo/deptemp/view/DataBindings.cpx

Figure 4-15. *Creating a binding for a client method*

Conclusion

In this chapter, you have seen how you can extend the standard functionality of ADF business components with your own logic. In some cases, you override the normal ADF methods, add functionality, or even completely replace standard ADF processing. In other cases, you add your own logic to view objects or application modules and make this logic available to the user interface layer with client interfaces.

In the next chapter, you will see how to add business logic in the user interface layer.

CHAPTER 5

Presentation Logic

As you saw in Chapter 1, ADF handles all the basic functionality of getting data from the database onto the web page, accepting changes, and storing data back. It's not until you want something other than the default functionality that you need to start writing code.

This chapter describes how to add logic to the presentation layer. ADF offers several ways:

- Prebuilt UI component validators (declarative)

- Managed beans (server-side Java code)

- Custom client-side JavaScript

Prebuilt Validators

You saw in Chapter 4 that it is possible to add a lot of validation to business component attributes, both declarative and programmatic. But this validation happens on the server, necessitating a server roundtrip. Some types of validation are so simple that they can be handled by client-side JavaScript, and ADF offers several prebuilt validators.

You find these in the *Components* window under the *Operations* heading near the bottom. They are shown in Figure 5-1.

© Sten Vesterli 2017
S. Vesterli, *Oracle ADF Survival Guide*, DOI 10.1007/978-1-4842-2820-3_5

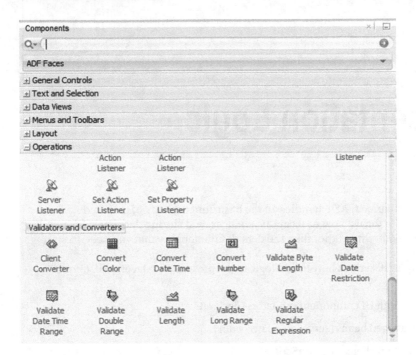

Figure 5-1. *Declarative validators for UI components*

To use one of these, you simply drop them onto a relevant UI component, for example, an *Input Text*. When you have done this, they will appear in the Source view of the page, as shown in Listing 5-1.

Listing 5-1. Example of Declarative Validator in Page Source

```xml
<?xml version='1.0' encoding='UTF-8'?>
<ui:composition xmlns:ui=http://java.sun.com/jsf/facelets
    xmlns:af="http://xmlns.oracle.com/adf/faces/rich"
    xmlns:f="http://java.sun.com/jsf/core">
  <af:pageTemplate viewId="/HrDemoPageFragmentTemplate.jsf" id="pt1">
    <f:facet name="content">
      <af:panelFormLayout id="pfl1">
...
        <af:inputText value="#{bindings.CommissionPct.inputValue}"
            label="#{bindings.CommissionPct.hints.label}"
            required="#{bindings.CommissionPct.hints.mandatory}"
            columns="#{bindings.CommissionPct.hints.displayWidth}"
            shortDesc="#{bindings.CommissionPct.hints.tooltip}" id="it7">
```

```
    <f:validator binding="#{bindings.CommissionPct.validator}"/>
    <af:convertNumber groupingUsed="false"
        pattern="#{bindings.CommissionPct.format}"/>
    <af:validateDoubleRange minimum="0.0" maximum="0.5"
        messageDetailMaximum="Max commission is 0.5"/>
  </af:inputText>
...
    </af:panelFormLayout>
  </f:facet>
 </af:pageTemplate>
</ui:composition>
```

They also appear in the *Structure* window in the bottom left corner of the JDeveloper window, as shown in Figure 5-2.

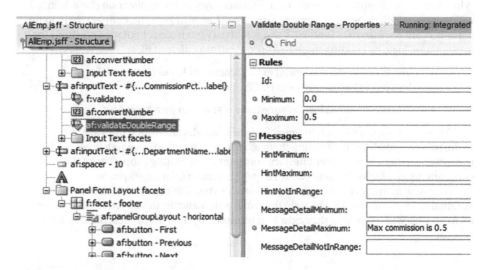

Figure 5-2. *Declarative validator in Structure window and its properties*

When you select the validator in either source view or the *Structure* window, its properties are shown in the *Properties* window. Here you can configure the validator and provide the message to be shown to the end user if the validation fails.

Declarative validations run on the client and are triggered as soon as the user leaves the field. Figure 5-3 shows the result displayed in the user interface when a declarative validation fails.

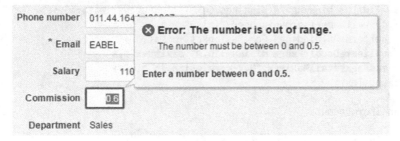

Figure 5-3. *Message to user when declarative validation fails*

Adding Managed Beans

When you need to apply logic in the user interface layer of the application (for advanced validations, calculations, etc.), you write managed beans in Java and connect them to the items on your page. In ADF (and JSF), the actual user interface is kept separate from the presentation logic by splitting these two functions into different files:

- The user interface is stored in the JavaServer Faces (JSF) and JavaServer Faces Fragment (JSFF) files

- The presentation logic source code is stored in Java bean files

Your application will contain many Java files. You declare which ones are part of the presentation layer by defining them as managed beans in your task flows, and then connect them to your user interface components by setting properties of the UI components to refer to the bean classes using *Expression Language* syntax.

The ADF framework *manages* these beans for you. This means that they are automatically instantiated at the right time, and automatically destroyed when they are no longer needed. How long they exist is determined by their *scope*, described in a later section.

Bean Classes

All classes you want to use in the user interface layer of your application must be valid Java beans. That means that they must

1. Have a public, no-argument default constructor.

2. Allow access to all properties with standard setter and getter methods.

3. Be serializable.

The *constructor* is simply a method with the same name as the class, taking no arguments. The ADF framework calls this method when it creates an instance of the bean class.

The setter and getter methods must be named in accordance with the JavaBean conventions. If for example the bean has a String attribute called firstName, it must have setFirstName() and getFirstName() methods.

■ **Note**   The attributes in your Java Bean source code must start with a lowercase letter.

That the bean is *serializable* means that it can be stored and deleted from memory, and later restored completely with all the internal state it had earlier. This is necessary for all beans you intend to use with a scope longer than Request.

■ **Note**   Short-lived beans (Request and BackingBean) will never have to be stored and restored, so they don't need to be serializable.

A typical bean that only contains attribute values and code can be made serializable simply by implementing the java.io.Serializable interface. Note that UI components and business components are *not* serializable, so you should not attempt to store these in your managed beans.

Bean Scope

You add managed beans to an ADF application by defining them as part of your bounded task flow. Whenever you add a bean, you also define its *scope*. If you are familiar with JSF, you will recognize Application, Session, View, and Request scopes, but ADF has more scopes. The following scopes exist in an ADF application, in order from the longest-lived to the shortest-lived:

- **Application:** Beans in application scope last until the application stops. This means they persist across user sessions—the user can close his browser and access the application days later and still find the same values in application scope. They are not cleared until an application server administrator terminates the application on the server (or it crashes). This can be used for application configurations you want to store in memory

- **Session:** Beans in session scope are created when the user first accesses an application and last until the user session ends—either because the user closes the browser or because the session times out due to inactivity. Session scoped beans are dangerous if the user should decide to run two instances of the application in the same browser. Some browsers will consider two instances of the application on separate browser tabs to be part of the same session, while other browsers will consider them two separate sessions.

- **PageFlow:** Beans in page flow scope are created when the user accesses the first page in a page flow and last until she leaves the page flow. They are useful in bounded task flows to store values that need to be accessible from all pages and other elements of the task flow. Page flow scope beans created in the unbounded task flow containing the master page are good places to store information you want to be available as long as the user is running the application. They are safer than session scope beans because they will always be separate for separate instances of the application, irrespective of how the browser handles sessions.

- **View:** Beans in view scope exist for the duration of a specific view (page or page fragment). Both JSF and ADF define a view scope; in an ADF application, you always get the ADF view scope when you refer to a bean.

- **Request:** Beans in request scope exist for the duration of one request (i.e., one server roundtrip). A bean in this scope can be accessed from all task flows on a page. This means that if a bounded task flow exists in two instances on the same page, a request scope bean is shared between them. This is normally not desirable, so you should prefer backing bean scope for short-lived beans.

- **BackingBean:** Beans in backing bean scope exist only for the duration of a request; this isolates separate instances of the same bounded task flow on a page. Use this scope for pure logic without state—code that needs to run in response to an event. As soon as the request is processed and the response sent back to the browser, a backing bean scope bean is terminated.

When you start out with ADF, try to limit yourself to PageFlow and BackingBean scopes: PageFlow for everything that needs to be stored for longer periods, and BackingBean for pure logic without state. This makes your code simpler and reduces the risk that one developer on your team stores something in one scope and another developer expects to find it in another.

Adding a Bean to the User Interface

JDeveloper offers you a couple of convenient shortcuts to add beans directly to the user interface elements on a page.

Adding a Bean to a Button

If you simply double-click a button in the *Design* view of a page in JDeveloper, the *Bind Action Property* dialog is shown. From this, you can either select an existing managed bean or click New to open the Create Managed Bean dialog shown in Figure 5-4.

Figure 5-4. The Create Managed Bean dialog

In this dialog, you enter a bean name and a class name. The bean name is used when referring to the bean in expression language expressions and the class name is the name of the corresponding Java file. By convention, the bean name starts with a lowercase letter and the class name starts with an uppercase letter. Beans related to a specific page (typically BackingBean scope) should be named after that page, and beans related to a whole task flow (often PageFlow scope) should be named after the flow.

You define the package your beans go into; by convention, beans go into a `.beans` subpackage under the base package of your view/controller project. Finally, you select a scope and leave the check box to create the class checked.

When you click *OK*, you are returned to the *Bind Action Property* dialog shown in Figure 5-4. JDeveloper will have filled in the *Method* field with something it has made up. Don't accept this default; click in the field and type a useful method name before you click *OK*. JDeveloper creates your class, which will look something like Listing 5-2.

Listing 5-2. Backing Bean Example

```
package com.vesterli.hrdemo.deptemp.view.beans;

public class EmpPage {
    public EmpPage() {
    }
```

```
    public String giveRaise() {
        // Add event code here...
        return null;
    }
}
```

If you look at the *Action* property for the button you clicked, you will find that JDeveloper has automatically filled it in with the correct value for the scope, class name, and method name you selected: #{backingBeanScope.empPage.giveRaise}.

If you look at the task flow your page or page fragment is part of, you can see on the *Managed Beans* subtab on the *Overview* tab that the bean has been added, as shown in Figure 5-5.

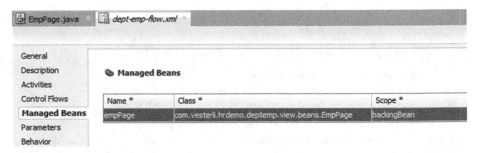

Figure 5-5. *A managed bean added to a task flow*

Adding a Bean to a databound Component

You can also add a bean by double-clicking a databound component like an *Input Text*. The Bind Validator Property dialog appears and allows you to create a new bean as shown in the preceding, or select an existing bean. You must provide a method name for your data validation, and JDeveloper will automatically place the method in your bean code and set the *Validator* property on the item.

For all UI components bound to business component attributes, it is normally better to place the validation on the business component. In this way, you only need to define the validation once and have it applied everywhere. If you decide to implement a custom validator in a bean, your bean code needs to throw a ValidatorException to indicate to ADF that the validation failed. One of the parameters to this exception is an instance of FacesMessage object containing the severity and the message text. Listing 5-3 shows an example of a validation method.

Listing 5-3. Validator Method in a Managed Bean

```
package com.vesterli.hrdemo.deptemp.view.beans;

import javax.faces.application.FacesMessage;
import javax.faces.component.UIComponent;
```

```
import javax.faces.context.FacesContext;
import javax.faces.validator.ValidatorException;

public class EmployeeBean {
  public EmployeeBean() {
  }
...
  public void salaryValidator(FacesContext facesContext,
      UIComponent uIComponent, Object object)
      throws ValidatorException {
    if (object != null) {
      int sal = Integer.valueOf(object.toString());
      if((sal % 10) != 0) {
        throw new ValidatorException(
            new FacesMessage(FacesMessage.SEVERITY_WARN,
            "Salary should be round number", null));
      }
    }
  }
}
```

Adding a Bean to a Task Flow

While the ability to add a bean and method directly to a button is useful, in most cases you need more control over the process. The normal way of adding a bean to a task flow is to first create the class and then add it to the relevant task flow.

You create the class like any other Java class. Then open the task flow where you want to use it and select the *Overview* tab and then the *Managed Beans* subtab to the right. Click the green plus sign, provide a bean name, point to the class and select a scope. When your bean is added, it looks as shown in Figure 5-5.

Interacting with UI Components

If your bean code needs to interact with UI components on the page, you need to create a component reference in the bean code and connect it to the UI components on the page. For example, you might want to add a new field for a suggested raise, and a button calling Java logic to read the existing salary and suggest a raise, as shown in Figure 5-6.

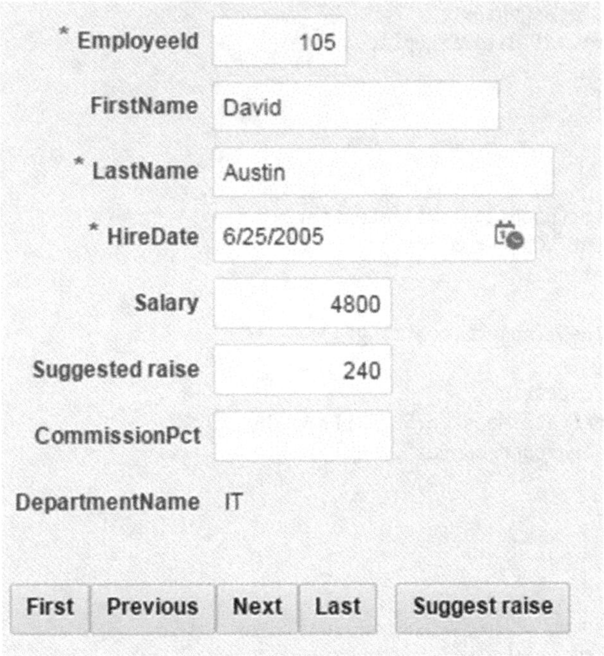

Figure 5-6. *Example of screen interacting with bean logic*

Creating a Component Reference

In the bean, you create a property that is an instance of ComponentReference, and setter and getter methods that use the class corresponding to the UI component. The name of the UI component class is generally "Rich" followed by the component name—for example, the RichInputText corresponds to an *Input Text* element. All of these classes are fund in subpackages under oracle.adf.view.rich.component.

■ **Tip** The full ADF RichClient API documentation can be found at *http://jdevadf. oracle.com/adf-richclient-demo/docs/apidocs/index.html.*

The code in Listing 5-4 shows an implementation of two component references: one for the input text element containing the existing salary value (e.g., from a business component) and one for another input text element that will contain the calculated raise. The SuggestRaise() method calculates 5% of the current salary and places that value into the suggested raise field.

Listing 5-4. Example of a Bean Manipulating UI Component Values

```
package com.vesterli.hrdemo.deptemp.view.beans;

import org.apache.myfaces.trinidad.util.ComponentReference;
...

public class EmpPage {
  private ComponentReference salary;
  private ComponentReference raise;

  public void setSalary(RichInputText salary) {
    this.salary = ComponentReference.newUIComponentReference(salary);
  }

  public RichInputText getSalary() {
    if (salary != null) {
      return (RichInputText)salary.getComponent();
    } else {
      return null;
    }
  }

  public void setRaise(RichInputText raise) {
    this.raise = ComponentReference.newUIComponentReference(raise);
  }

  public RichInputText getRaise() {
    if (raise != null) {
      return (RichInputText)raise.getComponent();
    } else {
      return null;
    }
  }

  public String suggestRaise() {
    BigDecimal orgSal = (BigDecimal)getSalary().getValue();
    BigDecimal suggestedRaise = orgSal.multiply(new BigDecimal(0.05));
    suggestedRaise = suggestedRaise.setScale(0, BigDecimal.ROUND_DOWN);
    getRaise().setValue(suggestedRaise);
    AdfFacesContext.getCurrentInstance().addPartialTarget(getRaise());
    return null;
  }
  ...
}
```

Note that getValue() in SuggestRaise() returns a generic Object. Because we are retrieving from salary, which is bound to a numeric field, that object can be cast to a BigDecimal. We then create another BigDecimal, do some calculations and rounding, and finally get the raise components and set its value.

It would be wasteful for ADF to automatically refresh the page every time an attribute changes. We must therefore explicitly ask for a component refresh, which we do by pushing it onto the list of objects to be redrawn with addPartialTarget().

You would only need to call setValue() on UI components that are not bound to a data source. If you want to change a value of a component that has a binding to a business component attribute, you should change the value of the bound attribute directly, as described in the section "Interacting with Business Components" later in this chapter.

Connecting the Bean to the UI Components

To connect the component references in the bean to the UI components, the *Binding* property of the components must be set to point to the bean attribute. To set the property, you can click the gearwheel icon to the right of the property and choose *Edit* to bring up the *Edit Property: Binding* dialog shown in Figure 5-7.

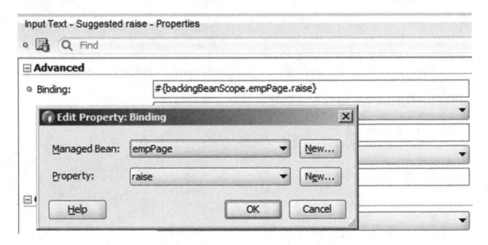

Figure 5-7. *The Edit Property Binding dialog*

When you select a managed bean, the *Property* drop-down will only display the attributes in the bean of the right type. In this example, you would need to set the *Binding* property for both the salary and suggested raise fields. To make the button call suggestRaise(), you'd have to set the *Action* property of the button as described previously.

> **Note** You can also create or select a bean and then click *New* next to *Property* to create a new property. If you do so, you will have to change the code slightly to include a `ComponentReference`, as shown in Listing 5-4.

Interacting with Business Components

When you want to work with business components from the user interface layer, you go through the binding layer. Don't try to access database data directly, because the rest of your application does use the binding layer. If one part of your application tries to circumvent the binding layer, you will get mysterious and hard-to-find bugs.

The Binding Layer

To see the available bindings on a page, you select the *Bindings* tab at the bottom of the page window. You will see a graphical representation of your bindings, as shown in Figure 5-8.

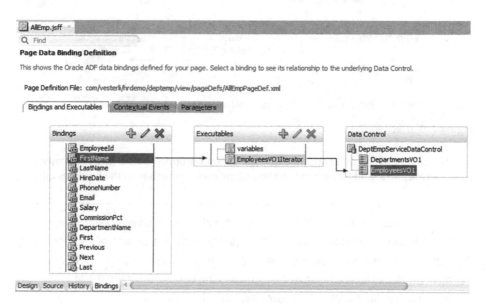

Figure 5-8. *Attribute value and action bindings*

ADF automatically creates bindings for you when you drop something from the Data Controls pane onto a page or page fragment:

- When you drop an individual attribute, you get an *attributeValues* binding and a single-attribute component like an *Input Text*. The FirstName binding on Figure 5-8 is an *attributeValue* binding.

- When you drop an operation, you get an *action* binding and an action component like a *Button*. The Previous binding on Figure 5-8 is an *action* binding.

- When you drop a whole view object instance, you get a *tree* binding and a multiattribute component like a *Table*. Figure 5-9 shows a *tree* binding.

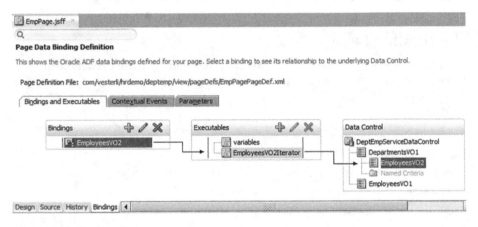

Figure 5-9. *Tree binding*

If you want to access an attribute that you haven't dropped onto a page, you must create an attribute binding by hand by clicking the green plus sign on the Bindings tab.

■ **Tip** If you want JDeveloper to help you, you can also try dropping an element on the page and then deleting the matching UI component *in the source view of the page*. If you delete the component from the *Design* tab or the *Structure* window, JDeveloper automatically cleans up and removes the corresponding binding. But if you delete a component on the *Source* tab, JDeveloper leaves the binding intact.

Accessing the Binding Layer

In order to access the binding layer from your code, the first thing you need to do is to create an instance of a BindingContainer, as shown in Listing 5-5.

Listing 5-5. Getting a BindingContainer

```
import oracle.adf.model.BindingContext;
import oracle.binding.BindingContainer;
...
public class EmpPage {
...
  public String processEmp {
    BindingContainer bc =
        BindingContext.getCurrent().getCurrentBindingsEntry();
    ...
  }
...
}
```

You normally don't have to type import statements when writing code in JDeveloper; the tool automatically provides suggestions. However, there are several options for both BindingContainer and BindingContext: you should choose the ones shown in Listing 5-5.

Getting the BindingContainer is something you'll be doing a lot in your code, so it makes sense to create a method for this in a utility class in your utility code project.

Accessing an Attribute Value

When you have a BindingContainer object, you can retrieve an attribute binding from it, as shown in Listing 5-6.

Listing 5-6. Getting Attribute Values

```
...
import java.math.BigDecimal;
import java.sql.Timestamp;

import oracle.adf.model.BindingContext;
import oracle.binding.AttributeBinding;
import oracle.binding.BindingContainer;
...

public class EmpPage {
...
  public String getEmpValues() {
    ...
```

```
    AttributeBinding fnb =
        (AttributeBinding)bc.getControlBinding("FirstName");
    AttributeBinding salb =
        (AttributeBinding)bc.getControlBinding("Salary");
    AttributeBinding hdb =
        (AttributeBinding)bc.getControlBinding("HireDate");
    String firstName = (String)fnb.getInputValue();
    BigDecimal sal = (BigDecimal)salb.getInputValue();
    Timestamp hireDate = (Timestamp)hdb.getInputValue();
    ...
    return null;
  }
}
```

The attribute name must be spelled exactly as written in the view object, with the exact same use of upper- and lowercase.

The signature of the getInputValue() method is that it returns a generic Object. However, ADF uses the object defined for the attribute on the *Attributes* tab in the view object, so you can cast the output of *getInputValue()* to the relevant type. The view object wizard in JDeveloper will create objects based on the *Data Type Map* setting defined when you initialize the model project for business components. When you use the default *Java Extended for Oracle* mapping, the following mappings occur:

- Database VARCHAR2 becomes java.lang.String

- Database NUMBER becomes java.math.BigDecimal

- Database DATE becomes java.sql.Timestamp

Accessing an Operation

As you saw in Chapter 4, business components come with built-in operations, and you can create your own operations. All the built-in operations and the operations that you have decided to expose to the user interface layer show up in the *Data Controls* pane in the *Applications* window.

■ **Tip**   If one of your custom operations doesn't show in the Data Controls pane, even after refreshing it with the blue double arrow icon, you probably forgot to create a client interface. See Chapter 4.

To execute an operation from managed bean code, you also go through the binding layer. The necessary code is shown in Listing 5-7.

Listing 5-7. Executing an Operation

```
...
import java.util.List;
import java.util.Map;
import oracle.adf.model.BindingContext;
import oracle.binding.OperationBinding;
...
public class EmpPage {
...
  public String changeDept(Integer empId, Integer deptId) {
    ...
    OperationBinding ob = bc.getOperationBinding("moveDept");
    Map obParam = ob.getParamsMap();
    obParam.put("empId", empId);
    obParam.put("deptId", deptId);
    Object result = ob.execute();
    if(!ob.getErrors().isEmpty()) {
      handleErrors(ob.getErrors());
      return null;
    }
    ...
    return null;
  }
}
```

Like the attribute binding, the name of the operation must be exactly as you see it on the *Bindings* tab, including use of upper- and lowercase.

Your operation might take one or more parameters. If this is the case, you retrieve a Map object from the operations binding and place your parameters in this map. If you don't have any parameters to pass, you don't need these lines of code.

Executing an operations binding always returns a generic Object; depending on the underlying code, that might or might not be useful in the bean calling the method.

You should always call getErrors() to check if anything went wrong when executing the operation. The return value from this method is a java.util.List object containing Throwable objects for any errors.

Accessing an Iterator

When you want to work with a whole data set, not just a single value, you need to access the iterator of a tree binding. To do this, you cast your binding container to a DCBindingContainer, as shown in Listing 5-8.

Listing 5-8. Iterating over a Data Set

```
...
import oracle.adf.model.BindingContext;
import oracle.adf.model.binding.DCBindingContainer;
import oracle.adf.model.binding.DCIteratorBinding;
import oracle.adf.view.rich.component.rich.data.RichTable;
import oracle.adf.view.rich.context.AdfFacesContext;
import oracle.jbo.Row;
...

public class EmployeeBean {
  ...
  private ComponentReference empTab;
  ...
  public void setEmpTab(RichTable empTab) {
    this.empTab = ComponentReference.newUIComponentReference(empTab);
  }
  public RichTable getEmpTab() {
    if (empTab != null) {
      return (RichTable)empTab.getComponent();
    } else {
      return null;
    }
  }
  ...
  public String DeptRaise() {
    BindingContainer bc =
        BindingContext.getCurrent().getCurrentBindingsEntry();
    DCBindingContainer dcb =(DCBindingContainer)bc;
    DCIteratorBinding iter =
        (DCIteratorBinding)dcb
        .findIteratorBinding("EmployeesInDeptVOIterator");
    Row[] allRows = iter.getAllRowsInRange();
    BigDecimal currSal;
    for (Row r: allRows) {
      currSal = (BigDecimal)r.getAttribute("Salary");
      r.setAttribute("Salary", currSal.multiply(new BigDecimal(1.05))
          .setScale(0, BigDecimal.ROUND_DOWN));
    }
    AdfFacesContext.getCurrentInstance().addPartialTarget(getEmpTab());
    return null;
  }
}
```

You retrieve the iterator binding from the container with findIteratorBinding(). Like all other bindings, you must type the name exactly as it exists on the *Bindings* tab. This iterator has a number of useful functions, one of which is getAllRowsInRange(), which returns an array of Row objects. In the preceding example, we simply loop over this array and give everybody a raise of 5%.

Changing the value of the attribute does not in itself update the UI component. To get the ADF table that displays the data from the iterator to update itself, we need to

- Create a ComponentReference for the table component

- Create setter and getter methods receiving and returning a RichTable

- Set the *Binding* property of the table to our RichTable property (with an expression like #{backingBeanScope.EmployeeBean. empTab})

- Add the table to the ADF Faces Context as a partial page rendering target with AdfFacesContext.getCurrentInstance().addPartia lTarget(getEmpTab());

Working with Selected Rows

If you want to work with the current record in the ADF table that displays data from an iterator, you might try the getCurrentRow() method that exists in the DCIteratorBinding object. However, that method returns the current row in the view object instance, not the currently selected row in the user interface. To access the selected row or rows in an ADF table component, you need to work with the table component first.

An ADF table has a property *rowSelection* that you can set to *none*, *single*, and *multiple*. When you drop a view object instance on a page, this is one of the selections you can make in the *Create Table* wizard, but you can of course always change it later. If you allow selection in a table, you can then retrieve the Key object for all selected records with the getSelectedRowKeys() method from the RichTable object connected to the UI component, as shown in Listing 5-9.

Listing 5-9. Working with Selected Rows in a Table

```
...
import oracle.adf.model.BindingContext;
import oracle.adf.model.binding.DCBindingContainer;
import oracle.adf.model.binding.DCIteratorBinding;
import oracle.adf.view.rich.component.rich.data.RichTable;
import oracle.jbo.Key;
import oracle.jbo.Row;
import oracle.jbo.RowSetIterator;
import org.apache.myfaces.trinidad.model.RowKeySet;
...
public class EmpPage {
  ...
```

```
  private ComponentReference empTab;
  ...
  public void setEmpTab(RichTable empTab) {
    this.empTab = ComponentReference.newUIComponentReference(empTab);
  }
  public RichTable getEmpTab() {
    if (empTab != null) {
      return (RichTable)empTab.getComponent();
    } else {
      return null;
    }
  }
  ...
  public String ProcessEmps() {
    RowKeySet selectedEmps = getEmpTab().getSelectedRowKeys();
    Iterator selIter = selectedEmps.iterator();
    BindingContainer bc =
        BindingContext.getCurrent().getCurrentBindingsEntry();
    DCBindingContainer dcb =(DCBindingContainer)bc;
    DCIteratorBinding empIter =
        (DCIteratorBinding)dcb.
        findIteratorBinding("EmployeesInDeptVOIterator");;
    RowSetIterator rsi = empIter.getRowSetIterator();
    Row curr = null;
    while (selIter.hasNext()) {
      Key key = (Key)((List)selIter.next()).get(0);
      curr = rsi.getRow(key);
      // process row
      ...
    }
    return null;
  }
}
```

When you have the set of row keys, you can get an Iterator object for the selected
rows. This is an iterator over *rows in the user interface* and has nothing to do with the
iterator connected with the view object instance.

To actually work with the data of the selected rows, you still need the
DCIteratorBinding as in the previous example. However, in this case, we get a
RowSetIterator from it. The advantage of this object is that it makes it easy to find a
specific row based on its key. As we loop over all the selected rows, we can retrieve the
Key and then use that to retrieve the actual row from the view object with getRow(key).

Interacting with the User

When a validation fails, you can use the default communication that ADF provides. This mechanism shows one or more messages and highlights any fields that fail validation. If you want more control over the messages displayed to your users, you need to create your own messages through using the JSF context. This object is created automatically and handles all the information around a server roundtrip.

Default Message

When you add your own messages to the JSF faces context, as shown in Listing 5-10, they are added to all the other messages your application wants to display to the user and displayed together in one dialog box.

Listing 5-10. Displaying a Message to the User in Default Position

```
...
import javax.faces.application.FacesMessage;
import javax.faces.context.FacesContext;
...
public class DeptPage {
  ...
  public String ShowMessage() {
    FacesContext fctx = FacesContext.getCurrentInstance();
    FacesMessage fm = new FacesMessage("General message");
    fm1.setSeverity(FacesMessage.SEVERITY_WARN);
    fctx.addMessage(null, fm);
    return null;
  }
  ...
}
```

As you can see, you create your message as FacesMessage objects with a message text and optionally set a severity. There are four severities available:

- SEVERITY_FATAL (not often used; a fatal error typically crashes the application)

- SEVERITY_ERROR

- SEVERITY_WARN

- SEVERITY_INFO

When you add the message to the faces context with null as the first parameter, as shown in the preceding, the message is displayed centered in the upper half of the application window, as shown in Figure 5-10.

Figure 5-10. *Message in default location*

Message Related to a Component

If your message is related to a specific UI component on the page, you can provide the client ID of that item as the first parameter. Listing 5-11 shows this.

Listing 5-11. Displaying a Message to the User in Relation to a Specific Component

```
...
import javax.faces.application.FacesMessage;
import javax.faces.context.FacesContext;
import oracle.adf.view.rich.component.rich.input.RichInputText;
...
public class DeptPage{
  private ComponentReference dname;
  ...
  public void setDname(RichInputText dname) {
    this.dname = ComponentReference.newUIComponentReference(dname);
  }

  public RichInputText getDname() {
    if (dname != null) {
      return (RichInputText)dname.getComponent();
    } else {
      return null;
    }
  }
  ...
  public String ShowAnother() {
    FacesContext fctx = FacesContext.getCurrentInstance();
```

```
FacesMessage fm = new FacesMessage(FacesMessage.SEVERITY_INFO,
    "Summary", "This is the detailed message");
String dnameItem = getDname().getClientId(fctx);
logger.finer("Dname field is " + dnameItem);
fctx.addMessage(dnameItem, fm);
return null;
  }
  ...
}
```

This requires that the component is connected to a bean property—in the preceding example, the *Binding* property of the department name item is set to #{backingBeanScope.deptPage.dname}.

Note that even though the first parameter of addMessage() is technically just a String, you can't just write the component ID here. You need the full location of the component, which depends on all the containers enclosing the component. The correct value will be something like pt1:r1:0:pt1:it2, so you should let getClientId() handle that for you.

When you place the message together with the component, it looks as shown in Figure 5-11.

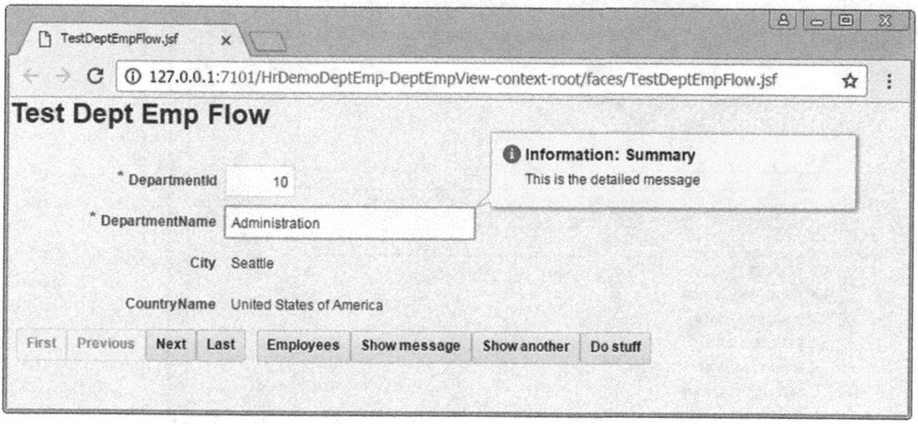

Figure 5-11. *Message aligned with UI component*

It is possible to add both general and component-aligned messages to a page. ADF does its best to show all of them, but the result is confusing to most users. If you are going to add your own messages, use only one position.

Using a Message Area

If you don't want your general messages displayed in a pop-up window, you can also add an inline *Messages* component (`<af:messages inline="true">`) somewhere on your page. All general (not component aligned) ADF messages will then be displayed in this area.

Logic in Task Flows

With managed beans, you can implement custom behavior in your pages, but you can also add your own code to control behavior in task flows.

Calling Managed Beans Task Flows

If you want to run some code between two pages in your task flow, you drop a *Method Call* activity from the *Components* window onto the *Diagram* view of your task flow. Give your method call a name and set the *Method* property to point to the method you want to execute. You can click the gearwheel icon to the left of the field to bring up the *Method Expression Builder*. This allows you to click your way to the method you need, as shown in Figure 5-12.

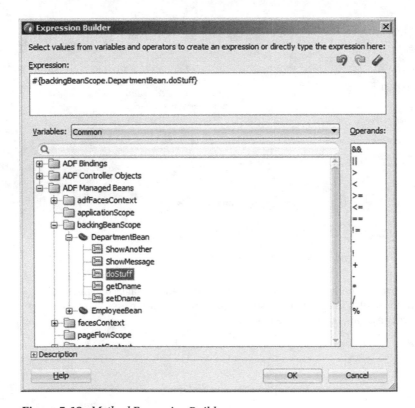

Figure 5-12. *Method Expression Builder*

When you have set the *Method*, you use regular *Control Flow Case* arrows to connect your *Method Call* to the other activities in the task flow. You need exactly one arrow going away from the *Method Call*, and the text on that *Control Flow Case* must match the value of the *Fixed Outcome* property.

Using Business Logic in Task Flows

You can also add logic from business components. Every operation shown in the *Data Controls* pane in the *Applications* window can be dragged onto the *Diagram* view and automatically becomes a *Method Call* activity. JDeveloper automatically establishes a binding if it doesn't already exist, and sets the *Method* property to match. The value will be something like #{binding. CreateWithParams.execute}.

Remember that you can add your own methods to ADF business components. If you have selected to create a *Client Interface* for your method, it shows up in the *Data Control* pane and can be used just like the built-in ADF operations.

How to Use Router Components

Method Call activities always have one outcome and the task flow follows the matching arrow to the next activity. However, you can make branching decisions in task flows using a *Router* activity.

A *Router* can have any number of *Control Flow Cases* leading away to other activities. One of these must match the *Default Outcome* property of the *Router*. In addition to this, you can define a number of *Cases*, each matching an *Expression* to an *Outcome* (arrow).

The expressions are written in Expression Language with the #{ ... } syntax, or you can use the *Expression Builder* to click together an expression. Notice that the *Expression Builder* contains operands you can use to compare values.

■ **Tip**   A literal value in Expression Language is written with single quotes inside the curly brackets, like this: #{'This is a literal value'}.

For any logic more complicated than simple comparisons, it is normally best to create a method in a managed bean that does the necessary calculations. Expression Language quickly becomes hard to read.

Task Flow Switching Logic

In earlier chapters, we have seen that an enterprise ADF application is normally structured with a number of bounded task flows using page fragments and a master page containing a menu structure and handling security. To allow switching between task flows from a menu on the master page, we need a *Dynamic Region* component and some code.

129

How Dynamic Regions Work

When you drag a task flow onto a page, you are given the option to create either a *Region* or a *Dynamic Region*. For static test pages, you can just create a static *Region*, but in a master page that should be able to show different task flows, you need a *Dynamic Region*.

The UI component on the page is an `<af:region>` in both cases, but if you choose a dynamic region, JDeveloper will help you create the additional code necessary.

When you create a static region, JDeveloper just creates a task flow binding pointing to the fixed path of the task flow. This will look something like `/WEB-INF/dept-emp-flow.xml#dept-emp-flow`.

When you create a dynamic region, JDeveloper does several things:

- Creates a task flow binding pointing to a managed bean. This will look something like `${viewScope.PageSwitcherBean.dynamicTaskFlowId}`.

- Prompts you for a name for the bean controlling the region and fills the bean class with sample content.

- Adds the bean to the unbounded task flow of the view project.

Building the Master Page

When you have built the first two task flows, whether in one subsystem or two, you can create the master application and the master page with task flow switching.

First, you need to create a template for the master page. This is done in the foundation workspace. Your template needs two facets: one for a menu and one for the page content. Normally, you would use a *Panel Grid Layout* with two rows of each one cell, setting the height of the top row to a small value like 30 pixels for the menu. The second row should take up all remaining space, so its height should be *Auto*. In the top cell, place a facet for the menu, and in the bottom cell, place a facet for the content.

In accordance with the modular ADF application architecture, the master application needs to have access to all the components that make up the application. This means that you need to add all the ADF libraries from your foundation layer as well as the ADF libraries containing the subsystems to the master workspace.

When you have added all the libraries, create the master page based on the template. In the menu facet, drop a *Menu Bar* component and then add one or more *Menu* components. On the *Menu*, you then drop *Menu Item* components that correspond with the task flows you want to display.

When you have created the menu, you open the subsystem ADF Library in the *Resources* window, as shown in Figure 5-13. Under the *ADF Task Flows* heading, you see all the task flows in the ADF Library. Drop one of these onto the content facet of your master page and choose *Dynamic Region* to get JDeveloper to do the necessary work described in the preceding section.

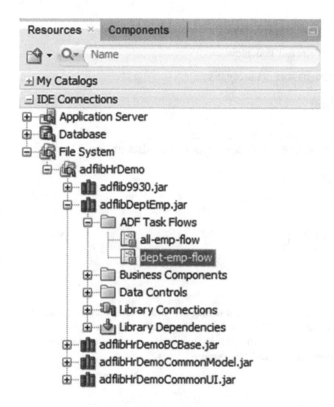

Figure 5-13. *The Resources window showing task flows from subsystems*

When you run this master page, you should see the page showing the menu and the one task flow you dropped on the page.

Storing State

The bean controlling the dynamic region has to be in *view* scope. This means it only exists while a specific page is being displayed, so it can't store which task flow is selected. For this, we need another bean with a longer scope. A good choice is to create a bean with page flow scope in the unbounded task flow in the master application. When the master application is started, the unbounded task flow starts, instantiates its page flow scope beans, and displays the master page. Because the unbounded task flow in the master application is active as long as the application runs, a bean in this scope will last as long as the application runs.

You need to create a state storing bean that looks as shown in Listing 5-12.

Listing 5-12. Bean for Storing Selected Task Flow

```
package com.vesterli.hrdemo.master.view.beans;

import java.io.Serializable;

public class UiStateBean implements Serializable {
  private String currentTF = "/WEB-INF/dept-emp-flow.xml#dept-emp-flow";

  public void setCurrentTF(String s) {
    this.currentTF = s;
  }

  public String getCurrentTF() {
    return currentTF;
  }
}
```

This bean simply holds a String variable containing the path to the selected task flow. It should be initialized with the first task flow you want your application to display.

You need to add this bean to the unbounded task flow (`adfc-config.xml`) in the view project of the master workspace in *pageFlow* scope.

Using Stored State

When you have a bean to store application state, you need to change the bean that provides the current task flow to the dynamic region. This bean already has some content that JDeveloper automatically created, but it should be changed to look like Listing 5-13.

Listing 5-13. Bean for Providing Task Flow ID to Dynamic Region

```
package com.vesterli.hrdemo.master.view.beans;

import java.io.Serializable;
import oracle.adf.controller.TaskFlowId;

public class PageSwitcherBean implements Serializable {
  private UiStateBean currentUiState;

  public PageSwitcherBean() {
  }
```

```
public TaskFlowId getDynamicTaskFlowId() {
  return TaskFlowId.parse(currentUiState.getCurrentTF());
}

public void setUiState(UiStateBean state) {
  currentUiState = state;
}
}
```

This bean now contains a private instance of the UI State bean and a method to set it. It still contains the getDynamicTaskFlowId() method created by JDeveloper, but the method now returns the string stored in the private UI state bean.

Connecting the Beans

In order to get ADF to pass the UI State bean to the page switcher bean each time it is initialized, we use an ADF feature called *managed properties*. All of the beans are managed beans; that is, the ADF framework creates and destroys them. But ADF can also manage the properties of these beans. This is done under the *Managed Properties* heading on the *Overview* tab of a task flow, as shown in Figure 5-14.

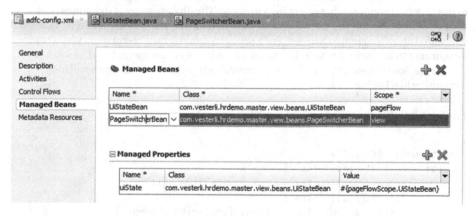

Figure 5-14. Using a managed property to connect UI state to page switcher bean

To set this property, first select the page switcher bean and then click the green plus sign next to *Managed Properties* to create a new managed property. Whenever the page switcher bean is created, ADF will automatically set the property. The setter method matching the *Name* of the property will be called with the content of the *Value* property. For example, if the name is uiState, ADF will call setUiState(). In Figure 5-14, you see that the *Value* is #{pageFlowScope.UiStateBean}. This means that the UiStateBean from the page flow scope is always inserted into the page switcher bean whenever it is created.

Connecting Menu Items

With all the code in place, we now need to actually set some values when the user selects a menu item. This is done by dropping a *Set Property Listener* component from the *Operations* section in the Components window onto each menu item. This brings up the Insert Set Property Listener dialog shown in Figure 5-15.

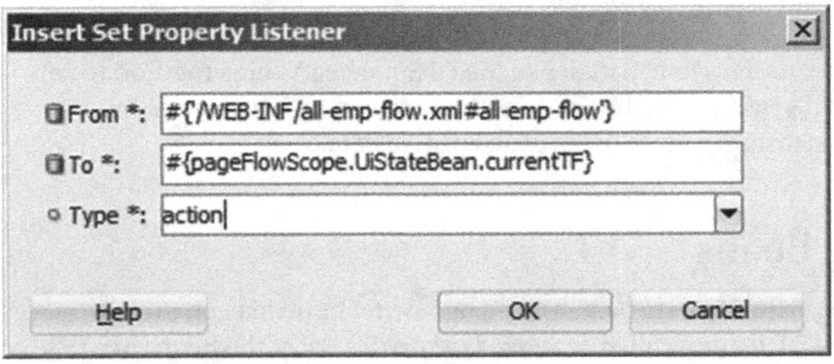

Figure 5-15. *The Insert Set Property Listener dialog*

The *From* parameter is a literal value as an Expression Language expression: the path to the task flow you want that menu item to show. The *To* parameter is the property in your UI state bean that you want the value assigned to, and the Action parameter is *when* you want the assignment to happen. For a property listener on a menu item, you want the assignment to happen on *action* (i.e., when the user selects the menu item).

In the Source view of your page, your menu with set property listeners will look something like Listing 5-14.

Listing 5-14. A menu with property listeners

```
...
  <af:menuBar id="mb1">
    <af:menu text="Employees" id="m1">
      <af:commandMenuItem text="Departments" id="cmi1">
        <af:setPropertyListener
            from="#{'/WEB-INF/dept-emp-flow.xml#dept-emp-flow'}"
            to="#{pageFlowScope.UiStateBean.currentTF}" type="action"/>
      </af:commandMenuItem>
      <af:commandMenuItem text="All employees" id="cmi2">
        <af:setPropertyListener
            from="#{'/WEB-INF/all-emp-flow.xml#all-emp-flow'}"
            to="#{pageFlowScope.UiStateBean.currentTF}" type="action"/>
      </af:commandMenuItem>
    </af:menu>
  </af:menuBar>
...
```

In this way, you can assign the paths to the different task flows to the UI state bean when the user selects each menu item.

Refreshing the Master Page

The final step is to ask the region to redraw itself whenever the value of the UI state changes. The region UI component doesn't know that you've changed the value of the UI state bean, so you have to tell it to refresh. This is done by setting the *PartialTriggers* property on the region.

When you click the gearwheel icon to the right of that property and select *Edit*, the *Edit Property: PartialTriggers* dialog appears as shown in Figure 5-16.

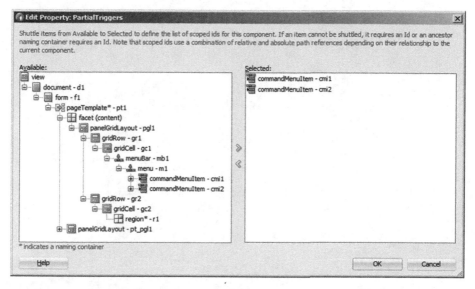

Figure 5-16. *The Edit Property: PartialTriggers dialog*

In this dialog, you specify the components that should trigger a refresh of the region. In the left side, you navigate to your menu item, select each one, and click the ➤ button to shuffle it to the right. Any action on an item in the *Selected* box to the right will cause the component to refresh as the user would expect from a modern web application.

When you run the master page, every time you click a menu item, the set property listener will store a new value in the UI state bean and tell the region to refresh. The region will refresh, asking the page switcher bean for the path to the task flow to be displayed, and the page switcher bean will read this from the UI state bean.

Conclusion

You have now seen how you can add presentation logic to your application to supplement the logic in the business layer to make your application do anything you need. But as always in programming, sometimes your code doesn't run correctly in the first attempt. In the next chapter, we'll discuss how you can use ADF's logging and debugging features to fix any problems with your code.

CHAPTER 6

■ ■ ■

Logging and Debugging

You've seen how to build an ADF application with powerful declarative features, and how to add your own business logic to both the business component and the user interface layer. However, sometimes your application doesn't work quite the way you expect it to. This is where logging and debugging comes into play.

Using ADF Logger

The first feature that helps you understand how your application works is logging. Java has basic logging features built in, and there are also several logging Java frameworks like Log4J. In an ADF application, you should use the ADF-specific ADFLogger class for your logging. The ADF Logger uses the standard Java logging API.

■ **Caution**   Don't ever use System.out.println() in production code, even if half the Java examples on the Internet do. You can't turn off this kind of logging, so you'll get an unmanageable amount of logging.

The ADF Logger has several benefits over standard Java logging, especially the fact that all log messages caused by the same ADF event are given the same Execution Context ID (ECID) so you can easily find all the log entries that are related to a specific message. You can also change log levels while the application is running, and even set a higher log level for a specific user of your application.

Adding Logging to Your Classes

All your Java classes should contain an instance of ADFLogger. In your team, decide on what you call it so that everyone can easily add new log statements everywhere in the knowledge that the logger exists. I recommend simply calling this instance logger.

© Sten Vesterli 2017
S. Vesterli, *Oracle ADF Survival Guide*, DOI 10.1007/978-1-4842-2820-3_6

You create it using the `createADFLogger()` factory method in the `ADFLogger` class, passing in the name of the current class, as shown in Listing 6-1.

Listing 6-1. Creating an ADFLogger Instance

```
package com.vesterli.hrdemo.deptemp.model.view;

import ...

public class EmployeesVORowImpl extends ViewRowImpl implements
EmployeesVORow {
  private ADFLogger logger =
      ADFLogger.createADFLogger(EmployeesVORowImpl.class);
  ...
}
```

If you don't provide the name of the current class, you will get a lot of log messages but will have no way to find out where the originated. Therefore, always provide a class name.

When you have a logger object in your class, you can add log statements to your code using the various methods offered by the `ADFLogger` class. All log statements have a log level, and it is important that your team makes a choice about how to use them. The following table shows my recommendation.

Log level	Used for
SEVERE	Critical errors that prevent the application from continuing. Your server administrator should set up monitoring of the ADF log files so that he and/or you get an alert if this happens.
WARNING	Warnings that indicate something wrong with the application. Often used to indicate misconfigurations, unexpected database errors, error messages, or no response from external systems.
INFO	Information for business users about what the application is doing.
CONFIG	Initialization of classes. Reading initial configuration from database or files.
FINE	Coarse-grained debug logging. Use FINE to log when methods are entered and/or exited (i.e., not more than twice in a method).
FINER	Medium-grained debug logging. Use FINER for more detailed logging inside methods.
FINEST	Fine-grained debug logging. Logging in loops should use FINEST.

In Listing 6-2, you can see some examples of ADF log statements.

Listing 6-2. Examples of ADF Logging

```
package com.vesterli.hrdemo.deptemp.view.beans;

import ...

public class EmpPage {
  ADFLogger logger = ADFLogger.createADFLogger(EmpPage.class);
...
  public String MultiRaise() {
    logger.fine("Entering MultiRaise()");
    RowKeySet selectedEmps = getEmpTab().getSelectedRowKeys();
    Iterator selIter = selectedEmps.iterator();

    logger.finer("Get iterator for all VO records");
    BindingContainer bc =
        BindingContext.getCurrent().getCurrentBindingsEntry();
    DCBindingContainer dcb =(DCBindingContainer)bc;
    DCIteratorBinding empIter =
        dcb.findIteratorBinding("EmployeesInDeptVOIterator");
    RowSetIterator rsi = empIter.getRowSetIterator();

    logger.finer("Loop over selected employees, give raise");
    Row currEmp = null;
    String oldSalString;
    BigDecimal oldSal;
    BigDecimal newSal;
    while (selIter.hasNext()) {
      Key key = (Key)((List)selIter.next()).get(0);
      currEmp = rsi.getRow(key);
      logger.finest("Working on " + currEmp.getAttribute("EmployeeId"));
      oldSalString = (String)currEmp.getAttribute("SalaryString");
      oldSal = new BigDecimal(oldSalString);
      logger.finest("Old sal is " + oldSal);
      newSal = oldSal.multiply(new BigDecimal(1.05))
          .setScale(0, BigDecimal.ROUND_DOWN);
      currEmp.setAttribute("SalaryString", newSal.toString());
      logger.finest("New sal is " + currEmp.getAttribute("SalaryString"));
    }

    logger.finer("Done increasing salaries, refreshing UI");
    AdfFacesContext.getCurrentInstance().addPartialTarget(empTab);
    return null;
  }
...
}
```

There is a single `logger.fine()` statement at the start of the method and a number of `logger.finer()` statements providing information through the flow of the method. Inside the loop in the second half of the code, `logger.finest()` is used.

Configuring Logging

The reason you want to use different log levels is so that you can apply relevant filters to your log. You can set the log threshold for an individual class or a Java package, and only the log statements that are at or above the threshold actually get written in the log. In this way, extra log statements are for all practical purposes "free," because the cost at runtime for a log statement below the threshold is so low.

By default, you will only see logs that are of level WARNING or higher. That is because your ADFLogger instances inherit their configuration from the Root Logger, which is set to WARNING. To see your own logs at different levels, you will need to add loggers named after your classes and packages and define their log levels.

This is done in the `logging.xml` file, but there is no need to edit this file directly. For the WebLogic server built into JDeveloper, you can click *Actions* and then *Configure Oracle Diagnostic Logging* from the *Log* window, as shown in Figure 6-1.

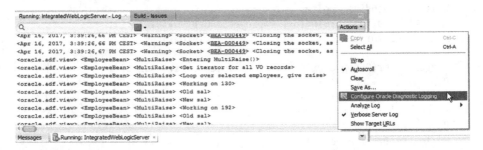

Figure 6-1. *Configuring ADF logging in JDeveloper*

This brings up the *logging.xml* file in JDeveloper. Because JDeveloper recognizes this file as a special configuration file, it provides an *Overview* tab where you can easily change log configuration. If you want to look at the raw configuration file, you can choose the *Source* tab at the bottom of the *logging.xml* window.

ADF has both *persistent* loggers that remain between invocations of your program and *transient* loggers created by ADF whenever an instance of a class with a log statement is instantiated. If you open the *logging.xml* window while an application is running in the built-in WebLogic server, you will see a lot of loggers. To get a better overview, check the *Hide Transient Loggers* check box, as shown in Figure 6-2.

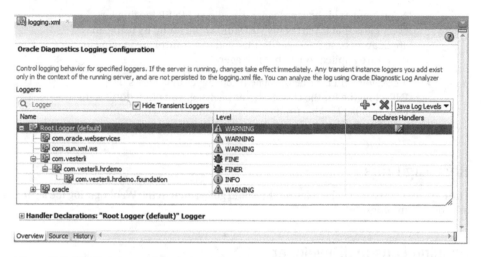

Figure 6-2. *The logging.xml Overview tab*

The loggers you add yourself should be *Persistent* loggers. To add these, click the green plus sign and choose *Add Persistent Logger*. In the dialog, enter a logger name and choose a log threshold.

- If your logger name is a package name, log statements at or above the threshold for every class in that package will be written to the log.

- If your logger name is the name of a specific class, only log statements at or above the threshold from that specific class are written to the log.

All the loggers are automatically arranged in a hierarchy below the *Root Logger*, and each logger can have its own log level. This gives you excellent control over what gets written to the log file.

For example, in Figure 6-2, I have specified

- A com.vesterli logger that allows FINE logging for every class where logging is not explicitly set by a lower-level logger. All the Java code produced by your organization should be under a similar base Java package.

- A com.vesterli.hrdemo logger that allows FINER logging for every class that is part of my HRDemo application. By using an application base package like this, you can control the logging for the entire application with one logger.

- A com.vesterli.hrdemo.foundation logger that shows only INFO logging for the classes in this package. You often don't want very detailed logging from your foundation classes once they are tested and used in your application.

Reading Logs

The log statements above the relevant threshold get written in the WebLogic log file and/or shown in the console.

Reading Logs in JDeveloper

As you run your application in the built-in WebLogic server in JDeveloper, you will see log entries appearing in the Log window. ADF doesn't distinguish between your log statements and the log that ADF itself produces. The default configuration of JDeveloper sets a fairly high threshold for the ADF packages, so you should not see a lot of ADF internal log information unless you add or reconfigure loggers.

■ **Note**   Even when you build your page by dragging and dropping components onto the page, you might get several ADF warnings. In effect, JDeveloper is complaining about the code it built itself. These warnings can safely be ignored. It is normally not worth the time to track down and fix the root cause.

Do not deselect the option called *Verbose Server Log* on the *Action* menu. This cuts down on logging output but doesn't discriminate between your logging and internal ADF logging, so you won't see any of your own logging either.

If you have a large log, you can use the *Oracle Diagnostic Log Analyzer* (ODLA) to examine it. To start this, you choose *Analyze Log* ➤ *Current in Console* from the *Action* button menu. The ODLA opens as shown in Figure 6-3.

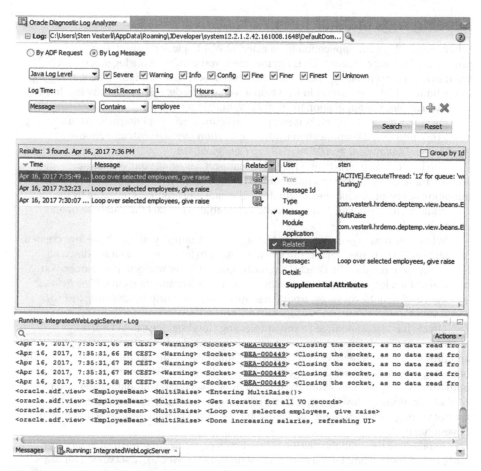

Figure 6-3. *The Oracle Diagnostic Log Analyzer*

At the top of the ODLA window, you can enter search criteria and execute a search. The most common search is to choose *By Log Message* in the radio group at the top. In the bottom row of search criteria, you will normally choose *Message* in the first drop-down and *Contains* in the second and then enter a search string.

In the results section in the lower part of the ODLA window, note the little triangle in the top right corner of the left-hand overview box. This allows you to select what attributes you want to see in the overview. If you choose *Related*, as shown in Figure 6-3, you get a column with a little icon.

This is a very powerful feature. If you click the little icon, you get a few options including *Related by Request*. If you choose this, you get every log message that was triggered by the same server roundtrip. This allows you to see everything that happened in all classes as result of the same user interaction (typically a mouse click or a keypress). Having the messages that came before the problem can often be very helpful, especially when all the irrelevant messages from other events are filtered out.

Reading Logs in Other Tools

When you deploy your application to an external WebLogic server for testing or production, the log configuration is not included. You configure the logging on each WebLogic server separately. This means that even if you have configured a lot of logging in the built-in WebLogic server in JDeveloper, you will by default not see any logging at all when you deploy the application to another WebLogic server.

On stand-alone WebLogic servers, you configure logging in Enterprise Manager. To do this, find the ADF application under *Application Deployments* and choose *Application Deployment* ➤ *ADF* ➤ *ADF Log Configuration*.

The logs can also be seen in Enterprise Manager, allowing your WebLogic administrator to see how your application is doing. Possibly, developers can even instruct operations personnel what they might do to alleviate any problems revealed by the logs. This could be the case if an ADF application is unable to contact the database or an external service.

When you view logs in Enterprise Manager Grid Control, you see all the logs created on that specific managed server. You will likely have to filter the log to track down an issue. Similar to the way the Oracle Diagnostic Log Analyzer works in JDeveloper, you can search for a log message that contains a specific string and then click *View Related Messages* and find the messages from the same server roundtrip by choosing *by ECID* (*Execution Context ID*).

Oracle has also announced a very interesting cloud service called *Oracle Management Cloud*. This cloud service can receive log files from all types of applications and present a comprehensive overview with visualizations and drill-down capability. One of the log inputs that Oracle Management Cloud will ingest is logs from ADF applications, both from ADF applications running on a WebLogic server in your datacenter and from ADF applications deployed to the Oracle Java Cloud Service. It was not released at the time of writing, but go to *cloud.oracle.com* and see if it is available and whether it would fit your needs.

Finally, you can read the raw log files yourself or configure some tool to monitor and present them. The ADF log entries are written to the WebLogic server log for the managed server you deploy your application to. If you deploy to a managed server called `MyManagedServer`, you find your ADF entries in the `MyManagedServer-diagnostic.log` file. Your server administrator can help you find this file, and can also use Enterprise Manager to move it to another location.

■ **Note** If you don't have access to the server file system, ask your server administrator if the log files from test servers could be placed on a shared network drive.

If you want to look at the log files from the WebLogic server built into JDeveloper, you find these in the domain home directory. On Windows, this will be something like `C:\Users\<your_user>\AppData\Roaming\<systemX.Y.Z>\DefaultDomain\servers\DefaultServer\logs\DefaultServer-diagnostic.log`.

Normal Debugging

JDeveloper is a complete Integrated Development Environment (IDE), so it, of course, contains all the debugging features you expect.

Setting a Breakpoint

To debug your Java code, you open the relevant class and click in the left margin to set a breakpoint. It is marked with a red dot and a red background behind the line with the breakpoint, as shown in Figure 6-4.

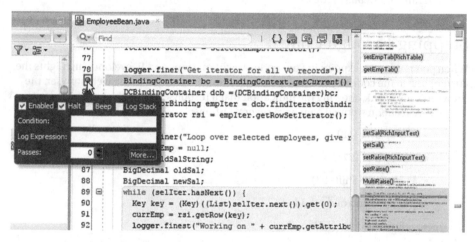

Figure 6-4. *Setting a breakpoint*

It is also marked in the right-hand margin with a small pink box, and if you are displaying the mini-map, the line with the breakpoint shows up as a pink line there as well. You can click in the mini-map or in the right margin to jump to a breakpoint (or any other point in the code).

■ **Note**   The Mini-map to the right in source view gives you a quick overview of large classes. You can right-click and set various settings and hide the map. To display it again, press Alt+Shift+period or choose *Source ➤ Show Mini-Map* from the right-click context menu in the source.

If you hover with the mouse over the red breakpoint dot in the left margin, you get a pop-up dialog, as shown in Figure 6-4. In this dialog, you can choose, for example, to stop only when you reach the breakpoint the fifth time or stop based on some condition. If you right-click the breakpoint dot and choose *Edit Breakpoint*, you get even more options to customize the breakpoint.

145

Running in Debug Mode

Once you have set the breakpoints you need, you right-click a runnable element and choose *Debug* (instead of the normal *Run*).

For task flows in subsystems, you normally run a test page containing the task flow you want to debug. To test the Java classes in your application, you will normally have unit test classes that invoke them, so you can just run these unit tests to invoke and debug your classes.

If the built-in WebLogic server is already started in normal (*Run*) mode, you will be prompted if you want to restart the server. Running in *Debug* mode is a bit slower and requires you to restart WebLogic, so JDeveloper protects you from accidentally changing between *Run* and *Debug* modes.

Stepping Through Code

When you reach a breakpoint in your code, execution stops and JDeveloper highlights the current line in the code. If you break before anything is returned to the web browser, the browser is just blank, showing the indication that a response has not been received yet.

With execution stopped, you have several options:

- Step over (F8)
- Step into (F7)
- Step out (Shift+F7)
- Step to end of method
- Run to cursor (F4)
- Resume (F9)

Some of these options are available from the toolbar above the source view, and all of them can be found on the *Source* menu.

The normal approach is to use *Step Over* to execute the code in your class line by line. JDeveloper shows execution times, some variables, and some control flow in the far left margin, as shown in Figure 6-5.

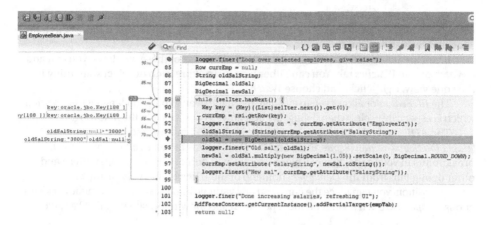

Figure 6-5. *Debugging code in JDeveloper*

By default, the far left margin (to the left of the line numbers in the regular margin) is rather narrow, but you can grab the edge of it to see more of the debug information, as shown in the preceding figure.

Step Into will step into the class that contains the method invoked by the currently open class. If the current line of code invokes methods from multiple other classes, you are prompted to select which class you want to step into. This is useful if you have a nested call hierarchy in your own code, but will sometimes just take you into the ADF source code from Oracle. Unless you have requested and installed the source code as explained later in this chapter, attempting to step into the ADF code will just give you an error about missing source code.

You can also just click to place the cursor further down in the code and press F4 to *Run to Cursor*. When you have gathered the information you need, you press *Resume* (F9) to allow JDeveloper to continue the execution.

Gathering Information

When you start the built-in WebLogic server in debug mode, JDeveloper automatically opens several new tabs for you in the *Log* window:

- Data

- Smart Data

- Watches

- EL Evaluator

- ADF Data

- Breakpoints

The *Data* tab shows information about all the objects currently memory in memory, while the *Smart Data* tab makes a guess at what is most relevant to you at this point in the code and only shows you this.

If you are interested in something that is not in either of these windows, you can add a *Watch* on the *Watches* tab. You can either type in an expression or select something in the code view, right-click, and choose *Watch*.

The *EL Evaluator* allows you to evaluate the value of an expression language expression, which is especially useful when debugging task flows as described in the following.

The *ADF Data* tab shows you everything in the ADF memory scopes (*pageFlowScope*, *requestScope*, etc.), and the *Breakpoints* tab gives an overview of all breakpoints in your code. You can close the tabs you don't need and reopen these and other debug tabs from the *Debugger* submenu of the JDeveloper *Window* menu.

In addition, you can place the cursor on any variable and press Ctrl+I (or right-click and choose *Inspect*) to open an independent pop-up *Inspector* window showing that variable.

Debugging Task Flows

Debugging code works when you can figure out which code is causing the problem. But sometimes, it can be hard to find the code that is running, or the execution flow through the application takes a different path from what you expect. Fortunately, JDeveloper offers you the ability to debug at a higher level than code: in the task flows.

To debug a task flow, you open it in the *Diagram* view and right-click a task flow activity. It gets a little red dot, as shown in Figure 6-6.

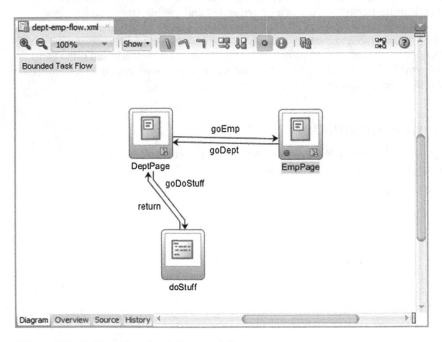

Figure 6-6. *Setting a breakpoint in a task flow*

When you run the application, execution stops at the breakpoint in the task flow. In JDeveloper, focus is on the task flow diagram with the active breakpoint, and JDeveloper is often moved to the foreground of your development machine (in front of the active browser window).

When you have stopped execution in a task flow, there isn't really any code to step through, but you can examine the state of the application using expression language (EL). You do this on the Expression Language tab in the Log window, as shown in Figure 6-7.

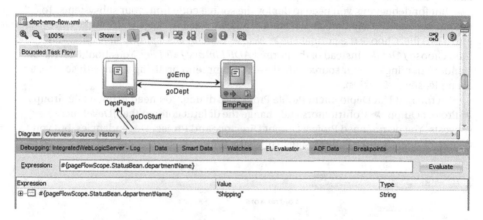

Figure 6-7. *Evaluating Expression Language when debugging task flow*

From this window, you can check values in managed beans and ADF internal values exposed as EL. Examples:

- `#{pageFlowScope.myBean.myAttribute}` will give you the value of the attribute `myAttribute` in the bean `myBean` in page flow scope. Note that if you choose the wrong scope, the expression language will just evaluate to null.

- `#{securityContext.userName}` will give you the name of the currently logged-in user. If the user has not logged in, this value will evaluate to `anonymous`.

- `#{facesContext.viewRoot.locale.language}` will give you the current language the application is running in (from the browser). This can be useful to debug translation or localization errors.

Debugging into ADF Libraries

As you saw in Chapter 2, an ADF application normally consists of several subsystems and a master application. Each subsystem is deployed as an ADF library, and the master application uses these libraries. But how do you debug a complete application when the bug you are chasing does not occur when testing the individual task flow? The solution is simple: you include the source code with the subsystems' ADF library.

Deploying Source Code

To allow the debugger to break in subsystem code and to display the relevant source code, it needs access to the source code. By default, an ADF library contains only the compiled Java class files (the bytecode), but not the source files. That is fine for deploying a production application where you don't want to bloat your libraries with source code the end user doesn't need. In some cases, your ADF application might even be used by an end customer that you don't want poking around in your source code.

But for debugging, you need to deploy the source code from your subsystems. To do this, you create a separate deployment profile that will package your source code into a JAR file. Choose the normal *File* ➤ *New* ➤ *General* ➤ *Deployment Profiles* and then choose *JAR File* (instead of the normal *ADF Library JAR File*). You should decide on standard naming for your source JAR files—I recommend prefixing them with source, for example, sourceDeptEmp.

In the Edit JAR Deployment Profile Properties dialog, you need to open File Groups ➤ Project Output ➤ Contributors and change the default content that JDeveloper suggests. You do not need Project Output Directory and Project Dependencies, but you do need Project Source Path, as shown in Figure 6-8.

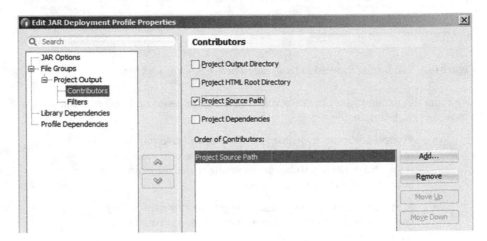

Figure 6-8. *Setting properties for a source JAR deployment*

Breaking in Library Code

When you have created source code JAR files for the relevant subsystems, you add them to your master application view project like any other JAR: *Project Properties* ➤ *Libraries and Classpath* ➤ *Add JAR/Directory*.

To see the source JAR file and set a breakpoint in it, you need to reconfigure the Applications window to show included libraries. This is done from the Navigator Display Options button in the top right corner of the Applications window. Select Show Libraries, as shown in Figure 6-9.

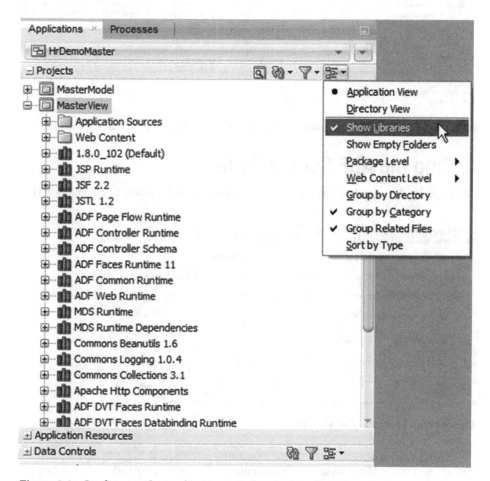

***Figure 6-9.** Configuring the Applications window to show libraries*

Now all libraries are shown in the Applications window. Find the source JAR file for the subsystem that you want to break inside, open it and double-click the Java file to open the source file. You can set breakpoints in these subsystem files, as shown in Figure 6-10, and when you run the master application, execution stops at the point you chose in the relevant subsystem.

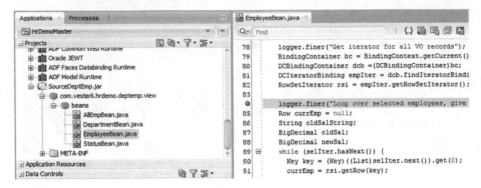

Figure 6-10. Placing a breakpoint in subsystem source code from the master application

Adding the ADF Source Code

When you are debugging ADF applications, you will often see the dialog box in Figure 6-11.

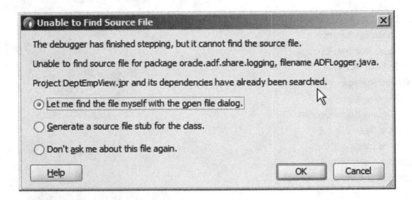

Figure 6-11. Unable to find source file

This dialog means that you wanted to continue single-line debugging, but JDeveloper couldn't find the source file containing the next piece of code to be executed. This can happen if execution continues into some of your own classes and you have not created a source code JAR as described in the preceding. But most often, it happens because execution continues into the large ADF code base delivered by Oracle. And by default, you don't have the Oracle ADF source code.

Getting the ADF Source Code

But if you have a valid support contract with Oracle, you can get the source code. The procedure is described in Doc ID 971256.1 on My Oracle Support, and the main steps are as follows:

1. You open a Service Request with My Oracle Support and ask for the ADF source code for the versions you need. You must supply the name, e-mail, and fax number (yes, really) of a person authorized to sign the Source Code Agreement (SCA) with Oracle. If you are a developer, this might be your manager.

2. Oracle sends you the SCA.

3. An authorized person from your organization signs and returns the SCA.

4. The SR is updated with a URL to the relevant source code ZIP and a password to open the ZIP file.

5. You download the ZIP file (it normally has a name like adf_vvvv_nnnn_source.zip, where vvvv is version number and nnnn is build).

Adding the ADF Source Code to JDeveloper

Once you have the ADF source code from Oracle, you normally create a user library for it. To do this, choose *Tools* ➤ *Manage Libraries* to bring up the *Manage Libraries* dialog. In this dialog, click *New* to add a new library for the ADF source. Provide a name and add the ZIP file as a new *Source Path* entry. Don't select the *Deployed by Default* check box.

Adding the ADF Source Code to a Project

When you have defined the ADF source user library, you can add it to each relevant project under *Project Properties* ➤ *Libraries and Classpaths* ➤ *Add Library*. Your ADF source library should appear under the *Users* node.

With the ADF source code part of your project, you can debug into ADF itself. You can also follow the execution path from your own application into the internal ADF classes if you need more information to help you debug a tricky issue. If you are curious about what ADF is doing internally, you can even set breakpoints in Oracle's code.

Tips and Tricks

When you have a problem with your ADF application, first run the *ADF Model Tester*. This will tell if you the problem is in the business components layer or the user interface layer.

If the Model Doesn't Run

Some types of errors mean that the model tester won't start at all. In this case, JDeveloper can't really offer any good advice, and all you see is in the Log window is something like Listing 6-3.

Listing 6-3. ADF Model Tester Incomplete Start

```
C:\Java\jdk1.8.0_102\bin\javaw.exe -server -classpath ...
Apr 17, 2017 5:31:10 PM oracle.security.jps.JpsStartup start
INFO: Jps initializing.
Apr 17, 2017 5:31:11 PM oracle.security.jps.JpsStartup start
INFO: Jps started.
Apr 17, 2017 5:31:20 PM oracle.jbo.jbotester.MainFrame main
INFO: BC4J Tester started.
```

If you don't see `jdev tester server connecting on port...` the model tester didn't start correctly. In this case, there is a problem with some of the code in your business components, and you need to check the source files for all your business components.

You need to open the XML file (on the *Source* tab for the business component) and any Java classes that you generated. A file with no problems has a green square at the top of the right margin and no other indications in the right margin, as shown in Figure 6-12.

Figure 6-12. A business component file without problems

If there is a problem with a file, the square at the top right is orange or red, and there will be orange and/or red lines in various places in the right margin, as shown in Figure 6-13.

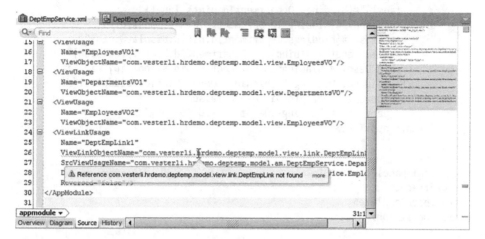

Figure 6-13. *A business component file with problems*

Each problem is highlighted in the code with an orange or red underline, and you can point to it to get JDeveloper to tell you what it thinks the problem is.

If the Page Is Empty

If your web page shows up empty, and the JDeveloper log doesn't tell you what is wrong, you need to examine the source file of the page. Look for errors and warnings marked with red and/or yellow bars in the right margin and underlines in the code.

If this doesn't help you, you can fall back to the time-proven way of debugging: commenting out code. Since the source of your page is XML, you need to use XML comment syntax of `<!-- -->`.

Start by placing a start comment near the very top of the page and comment out everything that contains expression language (bindings, action listeners, etc.). Then drop in some simple component from the *Components* window, as shown in Listing 6-4.

Listing 6-4. Commenting Out Parts of a Page

```
<?xml version='1.0' encoding='UTF-8'?>
<ui:composition xmlns:ui="http://java.sun.com/jsf/facelets"
    xmlns:af="http://xmlns.oracle.com/adf/faces/rich"
    xmlns:f="http://java.sun.com/jsf/core">
  <af:pageTemplate viewId="/HrDemoPageFragmentTemplate.jsf" id="pt1">
    <f:facet name="content">
      <af:panelFormLayout id="pfl1">
```

```
      <af:button text="button 1" id="b1"/>
      <!--
      <af:inputText value="#{bindings.DepartmentId.inputValue}"
          label="#{bindings.DepartmentId.hints.label}"
          required="#{bindings.DepartmentId.hints.mandatory}"
          columns="#{bindings.DepartmentId.hints.displayWidth}"
          maximumLength="#{bindings.DepartmentId.hints.precision}"
          shortDesc="#{bindings.DepartmentId.hints.tooltip}" id="it1">
        <f:validator binding="#{bindings.DepartmentId.validator}"/>
        <af:convertNumber groupingUsed="false"
            pattern="#{bindings.DepartmentId.format}"/>
      </af:inputText>
...
      -->
    </af:panelFormLayout>
  </f:facet>
  </af:pageTemplate>
</ui:composition>
```

Now, when you run your page, you should see only the simple component. Then move the comment start and end marks to include more and more of your UI components until you find the one that causes the problem.

Conclusion

You have seen how to add proper instrumentation to your ADF code and how to debug enterprise ADF applications. The last thing you need to know is how to implement a good workflow for effective enterprise ADF development.

CHAPTER 7

■ ■ ■

Your ADF Workflow

JDeveloper is an enterprise-level tool that supports and integrates with many of the tools
you need to support an enterprise application development process.

Work Process

Because ADF provides for so many ways of implementing common functionality once
and then sharing it across one or more applications, it is important that you set up your
project in the right way from the beginning.

Development work should happen on development workstations containing
JDeveloper and preferably a copy of the database. Modern workstations are powerful
enough that you can run JDeveloper, WebLogic, and a database at the same time, and
this configuration gives you much more flexibility when you are faced with the inevitable
changes to the database.

You deliver finished code to the central code repository, and a build process
(preferably automated) produces a version of the application and deploys it to an
integration environment.

Design Work

The first step is to design the application together with actual end users. Make sure you
have all kinds of users represented in the design group. It is a common problem that
applications are developed by expert users—this typically leads to overcomplicated
screens that are unintelligible by regular and novice users.

In addition to users, you need three different technical skills in order to produce
user-friendly applications quickly and efficiently with ADF:

- A User Experience (UX) designer

- An experienced Oracle ADF developer

- A database designer

© Sten Vesterli 2017
S. Vesterli, *Oracle ADF Survival Guide*, DOI 10.1007/978-1-4842-2820-3_7

The user experience designer facilitates workshops with the users to design screens and navigation that meet their needs while ensuring consistency and that UX best practice is being implemented. Oracle has researched user experience extensively, and has made all its best practices freely available. The UX designer on your team should familiarize herself with the Oracle Applications User Experience design patterns (www.oracle.com/webfolder/ux/applications/DPG/index.html) and read the free Oracle eBook for inspiration. If your ADF application is intended to extend Oracle's Cloud Applications, you should build your application in accordance with the *Simplified User Experience* guidelines so it looks like the applications in the Oracle Cloud Applications suite.

When the first draft of the user experience (screens and navigation) has been produced, the UX designer discusses it with the lead ADF developer. The developer can contribute to the design in two ways:

- By suggesting specialized ADF components that might provide additional functionality or convenience at little cost

- By suggesting alternative ways to meet a specific requirement if the suggested design will be hard to implement in standard ADF

The UX designer then makes any necessary changes to incorporate the input from the ADF developer and finalizes the design with the users.

When the design is done, the database designer works from the design to identity all data entities, along with their relations and attributes. At this stage, it might be necessary to go back to the users to clarify relationships, attributes, and valid values before the database is built.

Application Architecture

As the application specifications start to crystallize, you can start establishing the application architecture.

If this is the first ADF application you are building, you should start with a *modular* ADF architecture as described in Chapter 2, consisting of a foundation, several subsystems, and a master application.

If you already know that you will be building many ADF applications, and you have some experienced ADF developers on your team, you can also establish an *enterprise* ADF architecture from the beginning. This more complex architecture is also described in Chapter 2 and involves establishing both an enterprise foundation layer for all applications as well as individual application foundation layers for each application.

At this time, you need to decide on the number of subsystems, including names, scope, and Java package name for each.

Initial Development

Once the application architecture is in place, you can start the initial development. If you are running your project in accordance with an agile methodology, you might consider this the first sprint.

Development Standards

You need some place to document your development standards. To make it easy to update and track changes, this should preferably be a Wiki or similar, not a word processing document.

Your development standards must include Java package names for the foundation, all subsystems, and the master application. It should also include Java coding guidelines (fight the tabs-vs.-spaces war now and be done with it) and naming standards for ADF objects and Java classes.

■ **Tip** For inspiration to your ADF naming standards, you can look at the *ADF Naming and Project Layout Guidelines* developed by the ADF Enterprise Methodology Group (*www.oracle.com/technetwork/developer-tools/adf/learnmore/adf-naming-layout-guidelines-v2-00-1904828.pdf*).

JDeveloper has a long list of preferences you can set. Make sure you set at least the following:

- *Environment* ➤ *Encoding* (set to *UTF8*. Some JDeveloper versions on some platforms have another default)

- *ADF Business Components* ➤ *Base Classes* (set to your own BC base classes)

- *ADF Business Components* ➤ *Packages* (provide different subpackages for entities, associations, view objects, view links, and application modules in order to separate them in your code and in JDeveloper)

- *Code Editor* ➤ *Code Style* (duplicate a profile and adapt to your needs)

Create All JDeveloper Workspaces

With the standards in place, your lead developer or architect should create all the JDeveloper workspaces of your application, including the projects inside them. These workspaces should be created in a new directory not used for anything other than ADF workspaces and ADF libraries. We will refer to this directory as your *$ADF_ROOT* directory (e.g., C:\JDeveloper\hrdemo).

In a modular ADF architecture, this means creating

- The foundation workspace with projects for common model, common UI, common utility code, and business component base classes

- All the subsystem workspaces, each with a model and a view/controller project

159

- The master application workspace
- A directory to hold your ADF libraries

Create the Initial Foundation

Inside the foundation workspace, you should now create the elements that the entire application depends on:

- Business component base classes
- Page template
- Page fragment template
- Task flow template
- Application skin

Your business component base classes can be empty for now, but you need to create them and set up JDeveloper to use these base classes whenever you create ADF business components.

■ **Note** JDeveloper doesn't offer an easy way to move configurations from one JDeveloper instance to another, so there is no way to distribute a correct JDeveloper setup to your entire team, short of giving everybody a virtual machine with JDeveloper correctly installed.

Similarly, your templates and skin can be empty. Refer to Chapter 2 for more details on these elements.

When you have created this initial code, create ADF libraries from the common UI and business component base class projects. Place these ADF library JAR files in the common ADF library directories in your ADF project directory. Then place all your workspaces under version control and the ADF library directory under version control as described in the section "Source Control" later in this chapter.

Create the Database

In parallel with the work of creating JDeveloper workspaces and the initial foundation, your database design team can create the initial data model for your application.

A successful Oracle ADF project is based on a well-designed database. Database design is outside the scope of this book.

■ **Tip** It can be hard to ensure versioning of database objects like tables. Look at a tool like Flyway (*https://flywaydb.org/*) for one solution to handle the changes to the database that are inevitable in any project.

If you want to use JDeveloper to develop your database, look into the JDeveloper feature called *offline tables*. These are defined in JDeveloper and can be compared to an actual database, and JDeveloper can automatically create the necessary scripts to make the database look like the offline definitions.

Initial Application

The purpose of the initial application is twofold: you want to make sure that all the parts work together, and fix any issues before you start building in earnest. And you want to demonstrate to your users what the application is going to look like. In agile development, it is a basic tenet to be able to demonstrate some new functionality at the end of every two- or three-week sprint. Even if you are not implementing any other part of the agile methodology, it is a good idea to keep your users informed of progress by showing them regular demonstrations of the application.

Once the first version of the database is ready, you can create all the entity objects in the common model project using the *Business Components from Tables* wizard. Then create an ADF library from the common model project.

Then you build a simple subsystem implementing one screen from the application design. If your application contains screens for maintaining reference data, one of these screens might be a good candidate to implement in the initial application. The subsystem will involve a view object based on entity objects from the common model ADF library, and a task flow with a single page fragment. Deploy the finished subsystem as an ADF library.

In parallel with building the subsystem, your team should also build the master application with a menu and task flow switching logic as described in Chapter 5. If your application is going to implement ADF security, apply security to the master application now, using sample users for the demo.

■ **Note** Don't wait until the end of the project to implement security. If your application involves getting your WebLogic application server integrated with another identity provider like Microsoft Active Directory, you want to start this process early in the project so you have time to fix any issues that might occur.

Add the subsystem ADF library to the master application as described in Chapter 5 and test that you can invoke the task flow from the subsystem, and that you can make changes to data on the page fragment and store this changed data in the database.

Then show this basic application to your users. This gives them a first idea of what the finished ADF application will look like and proves to them that the project is progressing.

Constructing the Application

The initial application has proven that the entire technology stack works, or might have identified areas you need to work on (e.g., security integration). To build the rest of the application, you implement all the designed screens and other functionality in the subsystems.

If you are using an agile development approach, you choose a number of user stories for each sprint and continually deploy new ADF libraries from your subsystems and integrate them into the master application. If you are running your project in accordance with a traditional waterfall model, make sure to place some milestones in your plan where you integrate all of your work in the master application so you can demonstrate the current state of the application to the end users and other stakeholders.

Handling Database Changes

During development, there will always be changes to the database. There will be small changes to attributes within existing tables (new or modified columns), and maybe also larger, structural changes that involve new tables and changes to relations between tables.

When you need to make a small change to a table in the database, write a script to make the change in your local database. Then change the corresponding entity object in the common model project in the foundation workspace. You can right-click the entity object and select *Synchronize with Database* to ask JDeveloper to help you. The *Synchronize with Database* dialog appears as shown in Figure 7-1.

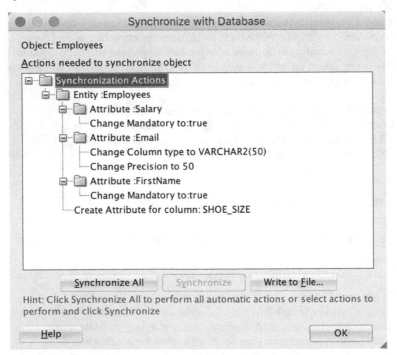

Figure 7-1. Synchronizing database changes with an ADF entity object

You need to click *Synchronize* or *Synchronize All* to ask JDeveloper to actually change your entity object—if you just click *OK*, no changes are made. After you confirm you want the change, JDeveloper confirms which changes were successful.

Note that attribute changes in the entity object are not automatically applied to the view objects using that entity object, and there is no corresponding "synchronize" feature for view objects. You must handle any view object changes manually. You can right-click the entity object and choose *Find Usages* to find the view objects that depend on that entity object.

Handling Other Foundation Changes

Changes to business component base classes should not break existing code. Similarly, changes to page and task flow templates might affect the visual appearance of the page, but should not break the application (unless you accidentally delete a facet used on some pages).

However, you should always perform a regression test to verify that your application still works. It is a good idea to automate application testing through the user interface.

Source Control

You need to keep your ADF application source code and libraries under version control. If your organization has worked with a tool like Oracle Forms that keeps all source organized in a few large files, you might have gotten by without proper version control until now. Once you start with ADF that uses a lot of small, but interdependent files, you absolutely need to implement source control.

The most popular version control software today is Git. Figure 7-2 shows a comparison of various version control tools over time from Google Trends.

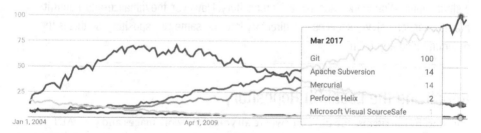

Mar 2017	
Git	100
Apache Subversion	14
Mercurial	14
Perforce Helix	2
Microsoft Visual SourceSafe	1

Figure 7-2. *Version Control software popularity*

Git is a free, open source tool that can be downloaded from `https://git-scm.com/` and run locally, or you can use a hosted instance like GitHub (`https://github.com/`). The Oracle Developer Cloud Service (DCS) described later in this chapter also uses Git. However, JDeveloper also has support for Apache Subversion built in, and you can download JDeveloper extensions for CVS, Perforce and others from the JDeveloper extension center at `http://apex.oracle.com/pls/apex/f?p=updatecenter:uc`.

Initial Versioning of an Entire Application

This section describes how to version an application using Git. Because Git is a *distributed* version control system, you normally commit changes to your private, local repository first and then *push* your changes to a central repository. Because Git is already integrated with JDeveloper, you don't have to download and install it.

■ **Tip** If you are using any Oracle Cloud service (like Java Cloud Service), the Oracle Developer Cloud Service (DCS) is included and available to you at no extra cost. This service includes a central Git repository and many other tools. If you plan to use DCS, refer to the specific section on DCS later in this chapter.

As mentioned earlier, your lead developer or architect should build all the necessary workspaces before development starts. He should also place all files under version control. This process involves four steps:

1. Initialize your ADF base directory as a local Git repository

2. Add all project files to this local repository

3. Commit all project files to the local repository

4. Push the local repository to a central Git repository accessible to all developers

---

■ **Note** If you use *Team ➤ Version Application*, the Import to Git wizard runs and versions a single application workspace into a Git repository. However, the initialize-add-commit method versions all workspaces in a directory into the same Git repository, so this is the recommended approach.

Initializing the Local Git Repository

You start by initializing the directory where all your ADF workspaces and your ADF library directory reside as a Git repository. A Git repository is just a directory with some extra files that Git understands. In this chapter, we will refer to this directory as $ADF_ROOT.

To do this, choose *Team ➤ Git ➤ Initialize*. This menu item is only active if you have a nonversioned application workspace open in JDeveloper. In the Initialize Repository dialog, provide the name of the root directory for all your ADF workspaces and the ADF library directory, as shown in Figure 7-3.

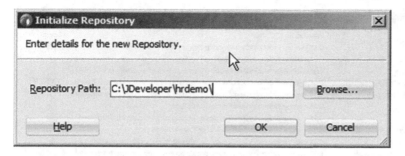

Figure 7-3. *Initializing the Git repository*

This adds a hidden `.git` subdirectory, turning the directory you specify into a Git repository.

Adding All Files

After this step, you will see in JDeveloper has added a little marker at the bottom left corner of the icons for all folders and files in the *Applications* window, as shown in Figure 7-4. If you point to a file or folder with the mouse cursor, the little pop-up field shows `Git: Unversioned`.

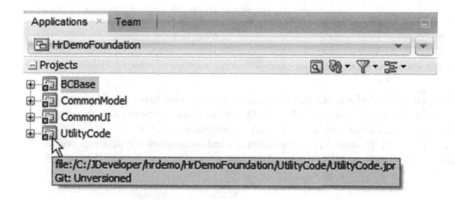

Figure 7-4. *Unversioned application workspace*

All the files in the workspace also show up in the *Pending Changes* window on the *Candidates* tab. If this window did not open automatically as a new tab next to the *Log* window at the bottom of the screen, you can open it by choosing *Team* ➤ *Git* ➤ *Pending Changes*.

To add all files, choose *Team* ➤ *Git* ➤ *Add all*. The *Add All* window appears and can be resized as shown in Figure 7-5.

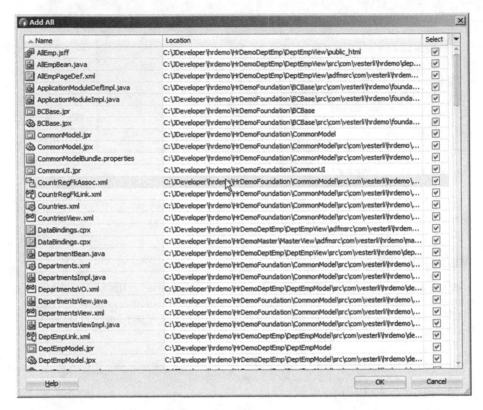

Figure 7-5. *The Add All dialog, expanded*

Notice that the *Add All* dialog includes all files from all workspaces under your *$ADF_ROOT*. Because you initialized the *$ADF_ROOT* directory as one Git repository, *Add All* works on all files in this directory and its subdirectories.

The marker on the icons in the *Applications* window changes to a plus sign and all files move to the *Outgoing* tab in the *Pending Changes* window, as shown in Figure 7-6.

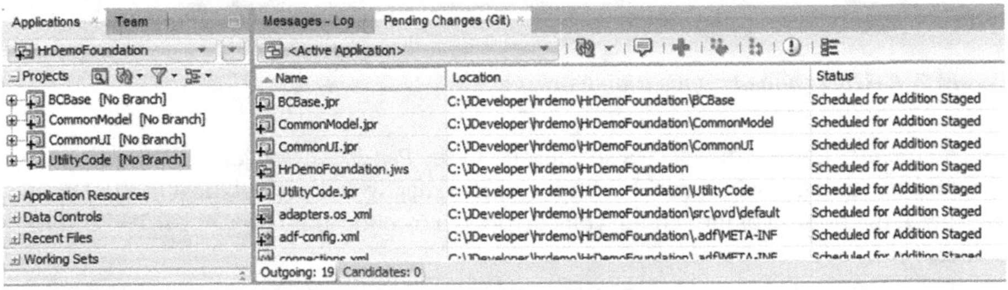

Figure 7-6. *Files added and ready to be committed to Git*

Committing All Files

To commit all files to your local Git repository, choose *Team* ➤ *Git* ➤ *Commit All* from the JDeveloper main menu or *Versioning* ➤ *Commit All* from the context menu in the *Applications* window. The *Commit All* dialog appears as shown in Figure 7-7.

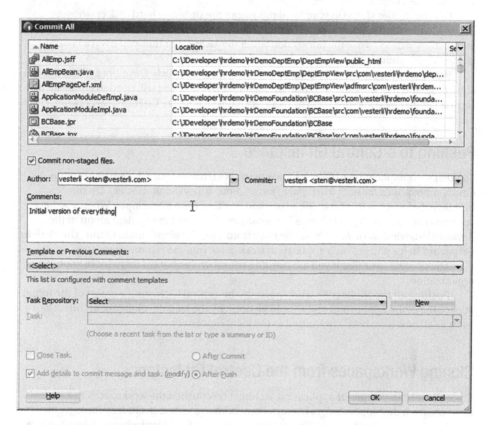

Figure 7-7. *The Commit All dialog*

Make sure you check the *Commit non-staged files* check box. Git actually works with a separate *staging area*, and files can be *Staged* or *Not Staged* (you can see this in the *Status* column in the *Pending Changes* window). Advanced Git users can use this feature to commit only some of the changed files by controlling whether they are staged or not. For everyday Git use, simply check the check box and commit all files whether staged or not.

Working with a Central Repository

When you commit files from JDeveloper, the change is stored in your local Git repository (the *$ADF_ROOT* catalog you initialized earlier). The fact that you work against the local repository makes commits very fast, and there is no risk that code you commit will break anybody else's code.

Of course, files stored in your local repository are only one hard disk crash away from oblivion, so you want to push your changes to a common repository for safekeeping and to allow others to use the latest code when they want. For this, you need a central repository for your team.

If you are using the Oracle Cloud, you have access to Oracle Developer Cloud Service at no cost, and that includes a central Git repository. If not, you will need to either set up a central Git instance for your team or use a hosted solution like GitHub (www.github.com).

Pushing to a Central Git Instance

To push your application to GitHub, you create a GitHub account, log on, and create empty repositories *for each workspace* (foundation, subsystems, master). Do not initialize them with a README file—they will be filled from JDeveloper. When you have your repositories ready, you choose *Versioning* ➤ *Push* from the context menu in the *Applications* window or *Team* ➤ *Git* ➤ *Push* from the JDeveloper main menu. The *Push to Git* wizard helps you get each application workspace into the remote repository.

The process is similar if you are running your own central Git instance in your organization.

Pushing all the application workspaces to the central Git instance is part of the initial versioning of the application and should be done by the lead developer or architect as soon as all files have been committed to the local repository.

Cloning Workspaces from the Central Git Instance

Once the lead developer or application architect has pushed the workspaces to a shared location, each developer can get his own copy from the server. In Git terminology, the developer *clones* the repository. To start the *Clone from Git* wizard, choose *Team* ➤ *Git* ➤ *Clone*.

Enter a remote name (by convention origin) and provide the URL to your repository. In step 4, provide the local directory where the local Git repository directory should be placed (your $ADF_ROOT). Because the cloning process will automatically create a directory with the same name as your Git repository, you should select the directory you want to be the parent of your $ADF_ROOT. For example, if your Git repository is called hrdemo, and you choose C:\JDeveloper as local directory, your Git repository directory becomes in C:\JDeveloper\hrdemo.

After downloading everything, JDeveloper will show you the ADF applications it found in the repository, and you can choose which applications you want to open in JDeveloper.

Getting Changes from the Central Git Instance

To download changes that other developers have pushed to the central repository server and merge them into your code, you use *Team ➤ Git ➤ Pull* from the JDeveloper menu. The *Pull from Git* wizard helps you download the changes. If you have merge conflicts that JDeveloper cannot resolve automatically, they will show up in the *Pending Changes* window, where you can choose *Resolve Conflict* from the right-click menu on each conflict to resolve it.

Git File Life Cycle

A file can have several different states in Git, as shown in Figure 7-8.

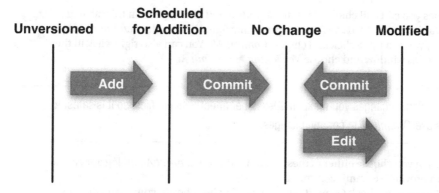

Figure 7-8. Git file status life cycle

When you clone the central repository to your local development workstation, all files will be committed to the local repository and have status *No Change*.

When you add a new file, it is *Unversioned*. It will also show up in the Pending Changes window on the Candidates tab, as shown in Figure 7-9.

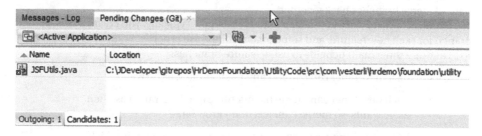

Figure 7-9. Pending Changes, Candidates

When you *Add* the file by selecting it on the *Pending Changes* tab and clicking the green plus icon, or right-clicking the file and choosing *Versioning* ➤ *Add*, the file moves to status *Scheduled for Addition*. It also disappears from the *Candidates* tab and appears on the *Outgoing* tab, as shown in Figure 7-10.

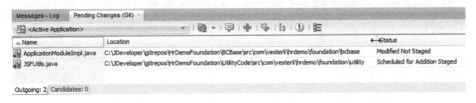

Figure 7-10. Pending Changes, Outgoing

Files you edit will change to status *Modified* and also appear on this tab (e.g., ApplicationModuleImpl.java in the preceding figure). From the *Pending Changes* window, you can right-click and choose *Commit All*. You can also right-click in the *Applications* window and choose *Versioning* ➤ *Commit All*.

■ Tip   Some changes you make in JDeveloper affect multiple files, so it is safest to always use *Commit All* to commit changes.

When you choose either of these commands, the *Commit All* dialog appears where you can provide a commit comment.

Make sure to check *Commit non-staged files* check box to commit all files. As mentioned earlier, Git has some advanced "staging" features, but you normally want to commit all files irrespective of their staging status.

Using Feature Branches

If you have worked with other version control systems before, you are probably very reluctant to create new code branches. And it has indeed historically been unreasonably hard to merge branches back together.

In Git, it is customary to use many more branches. Typically, you create a new branch for each new feature, and some organizations use separate branches for every bug fix. There are three main benefits to using feature branches:

- Each developer can commit and push as often as he wants

- Each developer can merge the mainline into his branch as often as he wants, so merge conflicts don't grow large

- When building a release, the release manager can decide which feature branches go into the release branch

Starting a Feature Branch

To start a new branch, choose *Team* ➤ *Git* ➤ *Create Branch* to bring up the *Create Branch* dialog, as shown in Figure 7-11.

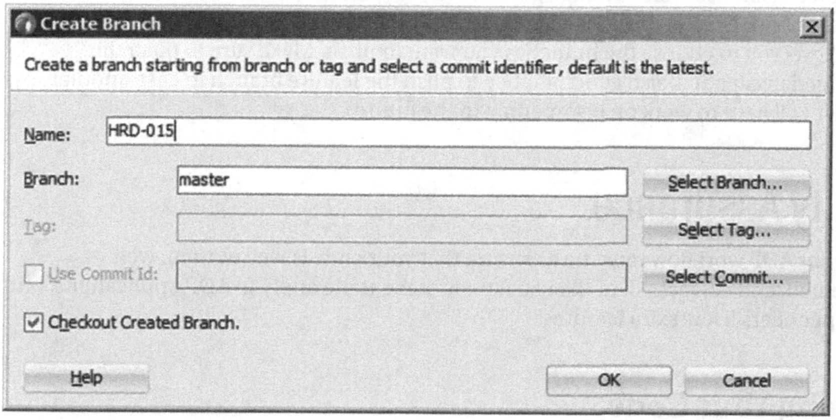

Figure 7-11. Creating a branch

Name your branch something short, but meaningful. The short name from your task/issue tracker is normally a good name. Make sure you leave the *Checkout Created Branch* check box checked in order to start working on your feature branch. You see the branch name in square brackets after each project in the *Applications* window now shows the name of your branch.

Working on a Feature Branch

Working on a feature branch is no different from other development work. You can commit freely to your local repository and should push to the central repository at least twice a day for backup.

While you are working, you might occasionally pull from the central repository if you know significant changes have been made to code you might be using.

Merging a Feature Branch

Once your feature is complete and committed locally, you switch to the master branch with *Team* ➤ *Git* ➤ *Checkout*. In the Checkout Revision dialog, you select the master branch (on the local node). You will see the branch name in the square brackets in the *Applications* window update to [master].

Then do a Git pull to get the latest changes to the master branch followed by a Git merge. In the *Merge* dialog, select your feature branch (under the Local node) and click *OK*. Normally, the merge happens automatically without error. If there are any merge conflicts, they will show up in the *Pending Changes* window marked with an exclamation mark. Right-click and choose *Resolve Conflict* to open the conflict resolution window, where you can choose which change goes in first, or manually create new merged code.

After the merge, you push the changes to the central repository. The *Push to Git* dialog allows you to choose the branches you want to push. Make sure to push the new merged master. It is also good practice to push the feature branch in case another developer will have to work on it sometime in the future.

Quality Assurance

Part of your ADF workflow must be to ensure that your code is well written, well documented, and correct. All of the usual tools of the trade apply to ADF applications, but JDeveloper offers a few extra features.

Auditing Your Code

On the *Build* menu, you find an entry called *Audit….* If you choose this, you are asked to select a profile and can then run an automated code audit. Note the *Edit* button—this calls up the *Audit Profile* dialog shown in Figure 7-12.

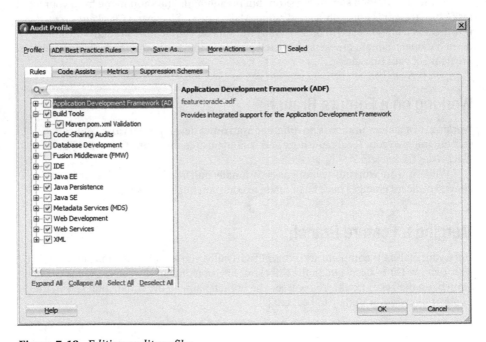

Figure 7-12. *Editing audit profiles*

In this dialog, you decide which rules are active in which profile.

When you run the audit, you get a lot of results in an expandable tree, as shown in Figure 7-13.

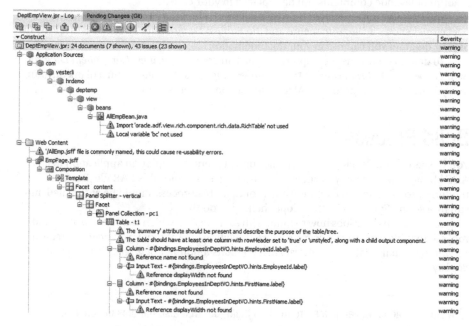

Figure 7-13. Audit result

In the toolbar above the result tree, you can change the display and turn of lower-priority issues. In a collapsed node in the tree, the value in the *Severity* column is the highest found in that node or its subnodes.

If you find that a specific warning does not help you, you can edit the profile to stop running that test. You can also hide all issues of a specific type by right-clicking one instance.

■ **Tip** Volunteers from the Oracle ADF Enterprise Methodology Group (ADF EMG) have developed extra audit rules specifically for ADF. See `https://adfaudit.atlassian.net/wiki/spaces/ADFAUDIT`

Documenting

JDeveloper offers to automatically produce Javadoc documentation for you if you choose *Build ➤ Javadoc ....* Naturally, the usefulness of the documentation depends on the amount of Javadoc comments you have placed in your code.

You can also document your visual task flows. When the *Diagram* tab is active, JDeveloper shows a *Diagram* menu, and the *Publish Diagram* menu item saves a PNG file of your diagram you can use in your documentation.

To document business components, you can create a *Business Component Diagram* with *File ➤ New ➤ From Gallery ➤ General ➤ Diagrams.* This gives you a blank diagram that you can drag and drop your ADF business components onto.

Build Process

You've seen how a developer can use the context menu to deploy an application to an ADF library, and to deploy the master application as a deployable EAR file. But in a modern, professional development environment, this process should be automated and run by a script. Fortunately, JDeveloper helps you do that.

This section describes how to build with Apache Ant, which is a very flexible build tool compatible with any project structure. To define an Ant build, you need to create a *buildfile* (normally called build.xml) that contains a number of *targets* like compile or deploy.

■ **Note**   Apache Maven is a more modern build tool that also handles dependency management, and from version 12c, JDeveloper also supports Maven. Since Maven assumes a standard directory structure that doesn't match the default ADF project, it takes some Maven skills to build ADF projects with Maven. If you have those skills, Maven is also a good choice as build tool.

Because the build scripts include directory names, including the complete path to where JDeveloper is installed, all developer workstations should be set up with JDeveloper and the *$ADF_ROOT* directory in the same location.

Building One Project

To build one project with Ant, you can choose *File ➤ New ➤ From Gallery ➤ General ➤ Ant ➤ Buildfile from Project.* The *Create Buildfile from Project* dialog appears as shown in Figure 7-14.

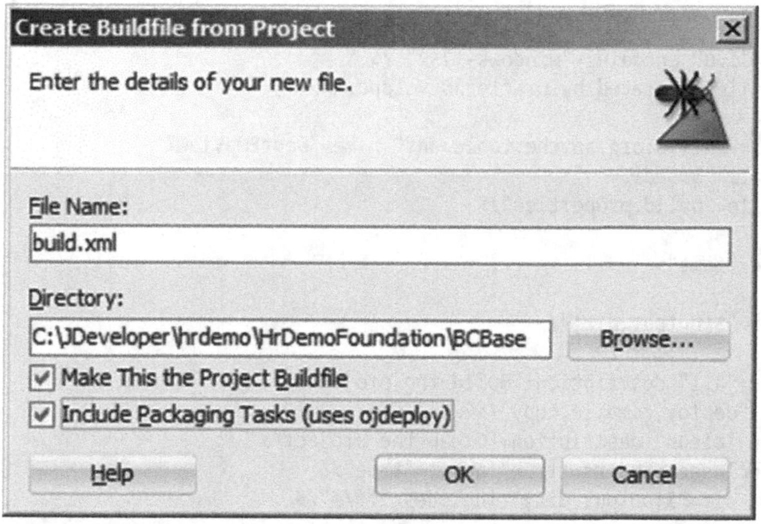

Figure 7-14. *Creating a buildfile from a project*

Make sure you check the *Include Packaging Tasks (uses ojdeploy)* check box. This option means that JDeveloper will include build tasks for actually packaging everything up into ADF libraries. The tasks that JDeveloper include in your build file depend on the *ojdeploy* utility installed with JDeveloper. There is currently no way to install only the *ojdeploy* utility on a build server, so you have to install JDeveloper on your build server in order to be able to use *ojdeploy*.

The autogenerated build file for a project will build all deployment profiles and all dependent projects. To build only what you need, you should delete any superfluous deployment profiles like the default profile created by JDeveloper.

In all ADF workspaces, JDeveloper by default registers a dependency from the view/controller project to the model project. The Ant build respects this dependency and automatically builds the model project when you build the view/controller. This means you only have to create an Ant build file for the view/controller project in each subsystem workspace.

When you create the buildfile for a project, JDeveloper creates a build.properties file containing various settings and directory names, and the build.xml file itself. These files show up in the *Applications* window under the *Resources* node.

The build.xml looks similar to the one in Listing 7-1.

Listing 7-1. Autogenerated build.xml File

```xml
<?xml version="1.0" encoding="windows-1252" ?>
<!--Ant buildfile generated by Oracle JDeveloper-->
...
<project xmlns="antlib:org.apache.tools.ant" name="DeptEmpView"
    default="all" basedir=".">
  <property file="build.properties"/>
...
  <target name="init">
    <tstamp/>
    <mkdir dir="${output.dir}"/>
  </target>
  <target name="all" description="Build the project"
      depends="deploy,compile,copy"/>
  <target name="clean" description="Clean the project">
    <delete includeemptydirs="true" quiet="true">
      <fileset dir="${output.dir}" includes="**/*"/>
    </delete>
  </target>
  <target name="deploy" description="Deploy JDeveloper profiles"
      depends="init">
    <taskdef name="ojdeploy"
      classname="oracle.jdeveloper.deploy.ant.OJDeployAntTask"
      uri="oraclelib:OJDeployAntTask"
      classpath="${oracle.jdeveloper.ant.library}"/>
    <ora:ojdeploy xmlns:ora="oraclelib:OJDeployAntTask"
      executable="${oracle.jdeveloper.ojdeploy.path}"
      ora:buildscript="${oracle.jdeveloper.deploy.dir}/ojdeploy-build.xml"
      ora:statuslog="${oracle.jdeveloper.deploy.dir}/ojdeploy-statuslog.xml">
      <ora:deploy>
        <ora:parameter name="workspace"
            value="${oracle.jdeveloper.workspace.path}"/>
        <ora:parameter name="project"
            value="${oracle.jdeveloper.project.name}"/>
        <ora:parameter name="profile"
            value="${oracle.jdeveloper.deploy.profile.name}"/>
        <ora:parameter name="nocompile" value="false"/>
        <ora:parameter name="outputfile"
            value="${oracle.jdeveloper.deploy.outputfile}"/>
      </ora:deploy>
    </ora:ojdeploy>
  </target>
  <target name="compile" description="Compile Java source files"
      depends="init">
```

```
    <javac destdir="${output.dir}" classpathref="classpath"
        debug="${javac.debug}" nowarn="${javac.nowarn}"
        deprecation="${javac.deprecation}" encoding="Cp1252"
        source="1.8" target="1.8">
      <src path="src"/>
    </javac>
  </target>
  <target name="copy" description="Copy files to output directory"
      depends="init">
    <patternset id="copy.patterns">
...

      <include name="**/*.xml"/>
      <include name="**/*.xsd"/>
      <include name="**/*.xsl"/>
      <exclude name="build.xml"/>
    </patternset>
    <copy todir="${output.dir}">
      <fileset dir="src">
        <patternset refid="copy.patterns"/>
      </fileset>
      <fileset dir=".">
        <patternset refid="copy.patterns"/>
      </fileset>
    </copy>
  </target>
</project>
```

You can see the target all depends on *deploy, compile,* and *copy.* This means that if you choose to build the *all* target, all the dependent build targets are also built. Most of these tasks use just standard Ant functionality documented at http://ant.apache.org/manual. The ADF-specific task is *ojdeploy*, found in the *deploy* target. This task point to the *ojdeploy* class necessary to build and sets the necessary parameters. The effect of this target is the same as manually building a deployment profile from within JDeveloper.

Building the Master Application

Before you create the build.xml file for the master application, you need to make sure you have a WAR deployment profile for the view/controller project, and an EAR deployment profile for the application.

The WAR deployment profile is created under project properties under the *Deployment* node in the same way subsystem ADF library deployment profiles are created.

The EAR deployment profile is part of the application properties. Choose *Application* ➤ *Application Properties* ➤ *Deployment* to create an *EAR File* deployment profile. Include the master view project on the *Application Assembly* node.

Once you have these two deployment profiles, create an Ant build *for the application*. This is done with *File* ➤ *New* ➤ *From Gallery* ➤ *General* ➤ *Ant* ➤ *Buildfile from Application*. The build file and the build properties file for the application show up in the *Application Resources* section of the *Applications* window, not under the project. You can build the complete application by right-clicking the build file and choosing *Run Ant Target* ➤ *deploy*.

Building Foundation and Subsystems

To build all the subsystems, you can add a new target to your master build file that uses <ant> tasks to call the Ant scripts from the subdirectories. If your buildfiles have the default build.xml name, you simply need to point Ant to all your foundation and subsystem directories. Your new target could look like Listing 7-2.

Listing 7-2. Ant Target Calling the Build Target for Foundation and Subsystems

```
<target name="buildsub"
    description="Build foundation and subsystems">
  <ant dir="${basedir}/../HrDemoFoundation/BCBase"
      inheritall="false"/>
  <ant dir="${basedir}/../HrDemoFoundation/CommonModel"
      inheritall="false"/>
  <ant dir="${basedir}/../HrDemoFoundation/CommonUI"
      inheritall="false"/>
  <ant dir="${basedir}/../HrDemoDeptEmp/DeptEmpView"
      inheritall="false"/>
  ...
</target>
```

Depending on your directory layout, you might need to tweak the references to the other build files. You can debug your Ant script by right-clicking it in JDeveloper and choosing *Debug Ant Target* and then your target. This gives you more verbose output you can use to find any errors.

The inheritall=false is an instruction to Ant to not send the master buildfile parameters to the subsystem builds, allowing the subsystems to use their individual build.properties files.

Copying ADF Libraries

All the foundation and subsystem ADF libraries are by default built in their respective deploy directories. You need to copy them to your common ADF library location by writing another target that uses ant *copy* tasks. This target could look as shown in Listing 7-3.

Listing 7-3. Ant Target Copying All ADF Libraries to Common Location

```
<target name="copysub"
    description="Copy foundation and subsystems ADF libs">
  <copy
    file="${basedir}/../HrDemoFoundation/BCBase/deploy/
      adflibBCBase.jar"
    todir="${basedir}/../adflibHrDemo"/>
  <copy
    file="${basedir}/../HrDemoFoundation/CommonModel/deploy/
      adflibHrDemoCommonModel.jar"
    todir="${basedir}/../adflibHrDemo"/>
  <copy
    file="${basedir}/../HrDemoFoundation/CommonUI/deploy/
      adflibHrDemoCommonUI.jar"
    todir="${basedir}/../adflibHrDemo"/>
  <copy
    file="${basedir}/../HrDemoDeptEmp/DeptEmpView/deploy/
      adflibDeptEmp.jar"
    todir="${basedir}/../adflibHrDemo"/>
  ...
</target>
```

■ **Note** The `file=` parameter in the preceding listing should be on one line: it is wrapped only because of the limitations of the book format.

Combined Build

Finally, you can modify the deploy target to depend on these two new tasks, like this: `<target name="deploy" depends="buildsub,copysub" ... >`. This ensures that they are always called before deployment, first `buildsub` and then `copysub`.

With this approach, you can build the entire application including all ADF libraries and the master application EAR with one Ant build instruction that can be run manually or integrated into any continuous build tool you might be using.

Using Developer Cloud Service

If you are using any Oracle Cloud services, the Oracle Developer Cloud Service (DCS) is included at no extra cost. This cloud-based service offers a comprehensive set of integrated development support features, including

- Git repository

- Code review workflow

- Task/Issue tracker

- Wiki

- Build server

- Deployment to other Oracle Cloud services

Other vendors like Atlassian or GitHub offer similar services, but since the Oracle service is free if you have other Oracle Cloud services, it might make sense for you to try it out.

Creating Users

The first step is to create your developers as users of the Oracle Developer Cloud Service. Starting from the *Sign In* link on http://cloud.oracle.com, you need to select which data center your cloud services are running in, along with your identity domain, and enter your username and password. All this information can be found in the welcome e-mail you receive from Oracle when you sign up for the Oracle cloud.

From the Oracle Cloud dashboard, you can click the *Users* button at the top right to define your developers as users of Oracle Cloud services. In the *Add User* dialog shown in Figure 7-15, make sure to assign the correct roles to your developers. To use Developer Cloud Service, your developers need the *Developer Service User Role*, and your lead developers and architects will probably need *Developer Service Administrator*.

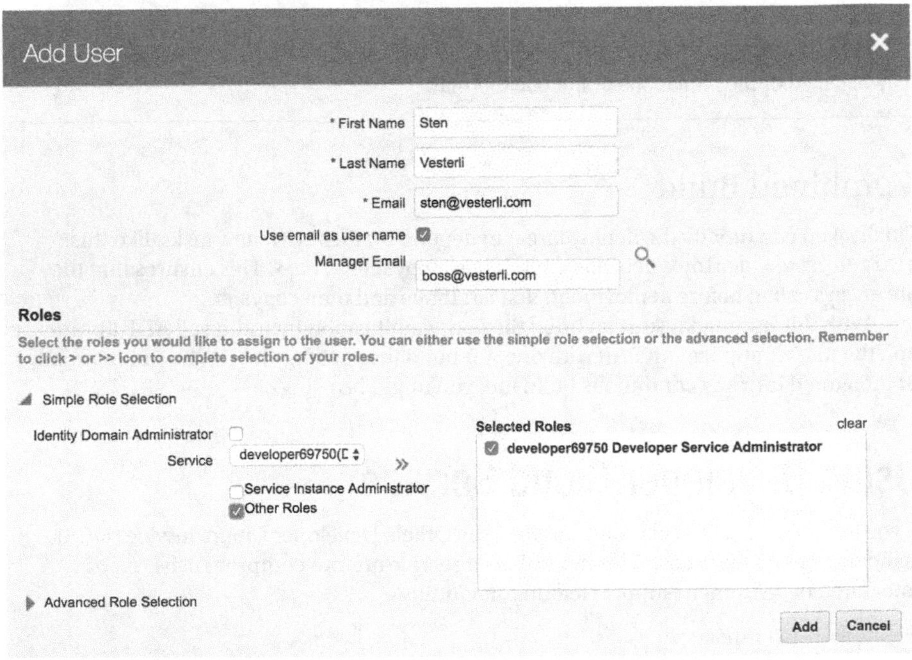

Figure 7-15. Assigning roles to Developer Cloud Service users

At the time of writing, this is not a very intuitive process. To assign the developer service user role, first select the developer service (called something like `developer69750`), then check the check box *Other Roles*, and finally click the ➤ link to assign that role to the user. To assign the developer service administrator role, you check the corresponding check box. Hopefully, this process will have been made more user-friendly by the time you read this book.

The newly created user now receives an e-mail with account information and a temporary password.

Creating Projects

Developer Cloud Service (DCS) can contain many independent *projects*. These are projects in the real meaning of the word, not the limited JDeveloper projects. You can create projects through the DCS web interface, but when working with multiple JDeveloper workspaces in a modular or enterprise ADF architecture, it is easier to create your project from JDeveloper. This is a task done once by the lead developer or architect once the initial workspaces are created.

Connecting to Developer Cloud Service

To begin, you need to create a connection to your cloud service instance from JDeveloper. This is done from the JDeveloper main menu under *Team* ➤ *Team Server* ➤ *Add Team Server*. In the New Team Server dialog, provide a name for your service and the URL. You can copy the URL from the welcome mail or your web browser—it will be something like `https://developer.us2.oraclecloud.com/developer12345-a667788`.

Then select *Team* ➤ *Team Server* ➤ *(your service name)* ➤ *Login*.

■ **Note**   To log on with a newly created Oracle Cloud user, you must log on through your web browser once to set your password and other authentication information.

Creating a Project

When you are logged in, choose *Team* ➤ *Team Server* ➤ *(your service name)* ➤ *New project*. The *New Project on Oracle Developer Cloud Service* dialog appears. In the first step, you provide a project name and a few other pieces of information. The *Private/Shared* setting controls if the project is only accessible to users who have explicitly been granted access, or to all users that are part of your identity domain.

In step two of the wizard, shown in Figure 7-16, you select the directory where you want your local Git repository to be placed, and select all the application workspaces you want to be part of this Git repository and Developer Cloud Service project.

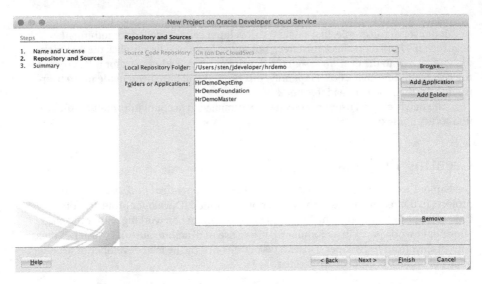

Figure 7-16. Adding application workspaces to Developer Cloud Service

In the final step, you are given a confirmation that explains that your application workspaces will be moved to the new local repository location. The process then runs for a while, moving the workspaces and creating a new project on the Developer Cloud Service.

When the process completes, you need to open one of the application workspaces from the new location. If you have any workspaces open from the original location, close these. The *Pending Changes* window will show the files in your workspace on the *Candidates* tab. Since the local and the central repository is Git, the same commands as described earlier apply: first you *Add All* and then you *Commit All*.

■ **Note**   Notice in the Commit All dialog box that your Developer Cloud Service is now automatically listed at the bottom under *Task Repository*. We'll get back to that later in this chapter.

When everything is committed to the local repository, do a *Push* to the central repository. When you look at your Developer Cloud Service instance from a web browser, you can now see your new project. When you open it, you see the project view shown in Figure 7-17.

Figure 7-17. *A project in Developer Cloud Service*

If you set your project to *Private*, you will have to add all relevant developers to your project on the TEAM tab (to the far right). If you set your project to *Shared*, all your Oracle Cloud users with the developer service user role can work on it.

Task Management

The Developer Cloud Service also has a task/issue tracking feature. You can create them from within JDeveloper in the *Team* window (where they are called *Tasks*) or through the web interface (where they are called *Issues*). JDeveloper automatically keeps the tasks in JDeveloper in sync with the tasks on the server.

The tasks have all the usual attributes, including priority, product, component, assignment, due date, estimate, time tracking, and so on.

One interesting feature is that you can add private details to a task, including notes and a date you personally schedule that task for.

If you use Developer Cloud Service, you should make use of this built-in task management, because you can choose a task each time you commit code to Git. This allows you full visibility into which code changes are associated with which task.

Working on Code

Developer Cloud Service uses Git, so the workflow is similar to the regular Git workflow described earlier in this chapter: create a feature branch and check it out, make your code changes in the branch, and commit regularly to the local repository.

When JDeveloper is connected to a Developer Cloud Service instance, the *Commit* dialog allows you to note which task the commit belongs to, as shown in Figure 7-18.

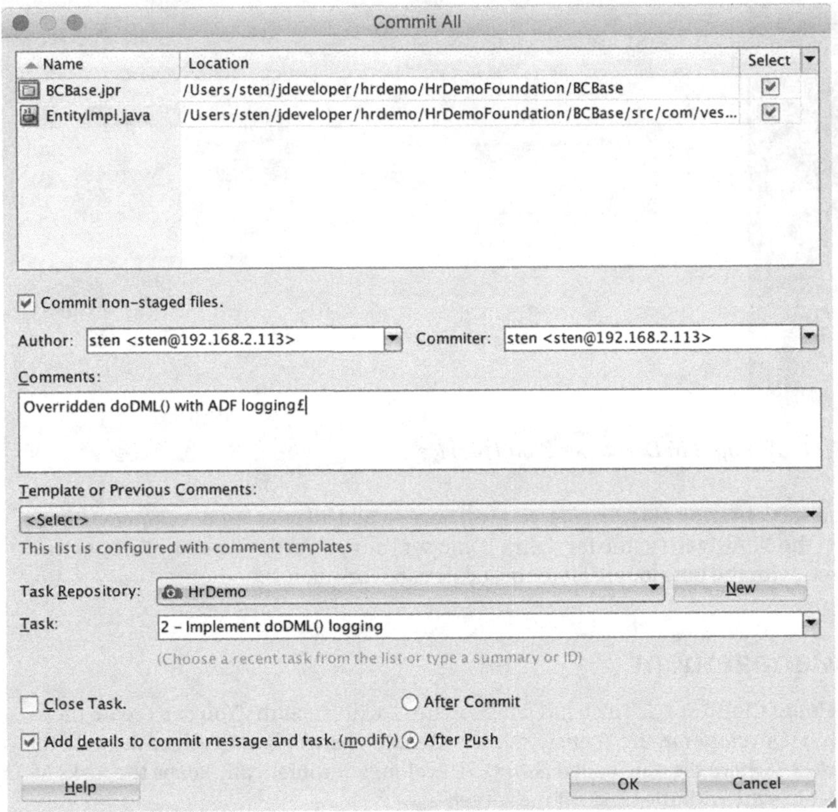

Figure 7-18. Commit dialog when connected to Developer Cloud Service

Note that you can select a task to associate with the commit. You can also choose to close the task when committing and/or add task information to the commit comment. You decide whether to do this as soon as you commit locally (*After Commit*) or not until you push the change to the central repository (*After Push*).

Code Review

When you are ready to submit your change to the central repository, you push your feature branch. Don't do a local merge when working with Developer Cloud Service.

When your feature branch has been pushed, go to the *Merge Requests* section on the DCS web pages and click *New Merge Request*. Select that you want to merge your feature branch with the master, as shown in Figure 7-19.

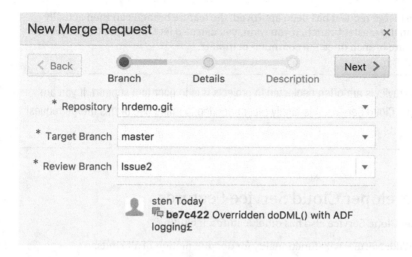

Figure 7-19. Creating a new merge request

In the second step of this wizard, choose the issue to link this merge request to, and select code reviewers.

The code review will now see this code request under *Assigned to Me*. When the reviewer opens it, he can see all changed files and commits and can comment either on the review in general or on specific code lines, as shown in Figure 7-20.

Figure 7-20. Commenting on a merge request

Once the merge request has been approved, the feature branch can then actually be merged into the master branch. If you want, you can also let Developer Cloud Service delete the feature branch once the commit is complete.

■ **Tip**   Code reviews are often neglected in projects due to poor tool support. If you are using Developer Cloud Service, it is highly recommended to make use of this merge request feature.

Other Developer Cloud Service Features

The Developer Cloud Service also has other features, including

- **Wiki:** Normal wiki functionality for documentation of all kinds.

- **Snippets:** The ability to store useful pieces for code, either privately for yourself or shared with other developers on the project.

- **Agile:** A couple of boards and reports useful when developing in accordance with agile methodology.

- **Build:** A build server where you can define jobs to automatically build and test your code. Offers various trigger points and build steps using Ant, Maven, SQL, shell scripts, and other tools.

- **Deploy:** The ability to define deployment configurations so you can automatically deploy your code to Oracle Java Cloud Service, for example.

Conclusion

Using the workflow described in this chapter, you can build high-quality enterprise applications. Together with the information from previous chapters about drag-and-drop building basic applications, enterprise architecture, user interface design, business logic, and logging and debugging, you are ready to work on real-life enterprise ADF applications.

Index

A

Accessors, 88
ADF EMG Task Flow Tester, 49
ADF Form layout, 26
ADF libraries
    containing ADF BC base classes, 35
    deployment profile, 33
    managing, 34
    refresh dependencies, 35
    using, 34, 74
ADF Model Tester, 8, 9, 153, 154
ADF skin, 48
ADF table layout, 26
Agile development approach,
    161, 162, 186
Apache Ant
    autogenerated build file, 175–177
    copy libraries to common
        location, 178–179
    create file, 174
    before deployment, 179
    EAR deployment profile, 177
    foundation and subsystems, 178
    ojdeploy, 175, 177
    WAR deployment profile, 177
Application development framework
    (ADF)
    binding layer, 3
    business components
        application modules, 4
        associations, 3
        entity objects, 3
        packages, 6
        view links, 4
        view objects, 4
    business services layer, 1–2
    high-level architecture, 2
    task flows
        bounded, 17
        unbounded, 17
    user interface layer, 2
    workspaces creation, 3
Application modules, 15–16
    view object instances, 15
Architecture models, ADF
    deploying, 39
    enterprise, 37–39
        application, 39
        master application, 39
        subsystems, 39
    modular, 35–36, 130
        master application, 37
        subsystems, 37
Associations, 3
    building, 10–11
Attribute value
    accessing from managed
        bean, 109, 119–120
    adding to page, 3

B

BackingBean scope, 110, 111
Beans
    BackingBean scopes, 110
    managed (*see* Managed beans)
    storing state, 131
    using stored state, 132–133
Binding layer, 3
    accessing from managed
        beans, 117–118
    action binding, 28, 118
    attribute binding, 28, 118
    tree binding, 28, 118
Bind variables, 14, 16

© Sten Vesterli 2017

S. Vesterli, *Oracle ADF Survival Guide*, DOI 10.1007/978-1-4842-2820-3

Get the eBook for only $5!

Why limit yourself?

With most of our titles available in both PDF and ePUB format, you can access your content wherever and however you wish—on your PC, phone, tablet, or reader.

Since you've purchased this print book, we are happy to offer you the eBook for just $5.

To learn more, go to http://www.apress.com/companion or contact support@apress.com.

Apress®

 **⟨IOUG⟩** *independent oracle users group* *For the Complete Technology & Database Professional*

IOUG represents the **voice of Oracle technology and database professionals -** empowering you to be **more productive** in your business and career by **delivering education,** sharing **best practices** and providing technology direction and **networking opportunities.**

Context, Not Just Content

IOUG is dedicated to helping our members become an #IOUGenius by staying on the cutting-edge of Oracle technologies and industry issues through practical content, user-focused education, and invaluable networking and leadership opportunities:

- *SELECT Journal* is our quarterly publication that provides in-depth, peer-reviewed articles on industry news and best practices in Oracle technology

- Our #IOUGenius blog highlights a featured weekly topic and provides content driven by Oracle professionals and the IOUG community

- Special Interest Groups provide you the chance to collaborate with peers on the specific issues that matter to you and even take on leadership roles outside of your organization

- COLLABORATE is our once-a-year opportunity to connect with the members of not one, but three, Oracle users groups (IOUG, OAUG and Quest) as well as with the top names and faces in the Oracle community.

Who we are...

... more than 20,000 database professionals, developers, application and infrastructure architects, business intelligence specialists and IT managers

... a community of users that share experiences and knowledge on issues and technologies that matter to you and your organization

Interested? Join IOUG's community of Oracle technology and database professionals at www.ioug.org/Join.

Independent Oracle Users Group | phone: (312) 245-1579 | email: membership@ioug.org
330 N. Wabash Ave., Suite 2000, Chicago, IL 60611

Printed in the United States
By Bookmasters